MEDITATION
IN MOTION

A must-read for those whose contemplation takes an active turn. I'm proud to say her ideas first appeared as an article in our magazine.

—Robert Owens Scott,
Editor in Chief, *Spirituality & Health*

Barbara Bartocci's inspiring true stories and practical how-tos will help you bring your soul along on your workout, and develop the inner *and* outer fitness that support each other. I highly recommend this book.

—Victoria Moran,
author of *Fit from Within:*
101 Simple Secrets to Change
Your Body and Your Life

If you want to play your best at the game that really counts in life, this is the right book for you.

—Joe Walsh,
Varsity Baseball coach,
Harvard University

Barbara's book is a wonderful compilation of stories and observations about the connection between physical and spiritual exercise. I recommend her book to anyone who would like to incorporate the two—both so vital for healthy living—into their own lives. . . .

—Amie Jew, M.D.,
surgeon.

exercise your body
and soul — at the same time!

MEDITATION
IN MOTION

barbara bartocci

 SORIN BOOKS™ Notre Dame, Indiana

www.avemariapress.com

International Standard Book Number: 1-893732-62-2

Cover and text design by K.H. Coney

Printed and bound in the United States of America.

Library of Congress Cataloging-in-Publication Data is available.

CONTENTS

HOW-TO

INTRODUCTION

from riding to writing. . . . .

I began to think about writing this book when I rose one summer morning at 5:30 and got on my bicycle. The sky was an iridescent hue of mother-of-pearl, and the Midwest heat was still held at bay. I headed for the country beyond our housebound suburbs, and as I pedaled, I drew in deep, slow breaths, relishing the organic smells. I paid attention to details—a white cat darting behind a house, roses in vivid bloom against brown wooden shingles, a dog yipping in a backyard, a man in a striped bathrobe sleepily reaching for his newspaper.

My wheels circled like prayer beads in rhythm with my breath. With each turn of my tires, it seemed natural—effortless—to recite a common prayer from my Catholic childhood: "Jesus, Mercy . . . Christ, have Mercy. . . ." The prayerful repetition brought a deep sense of oneness with my environment, and a feeling of harmony with the world that stayed with me the rest of the day.

sport and spirit: connecting the dots

The sense of connection felt new to me, but connecting the physical with the spiritual is actually as old as humankind is. Early cultures didn't distinguish at all between religion and sports or games. From Africa to the Americas, native cultures incorporated sports into religious rites. Primitive ball games were played for the purpose of directing the wind gods, or to encourage fertility. Groups of rainmaking priests might even be called the earliest teams.

In ancient Greece, Plato and Aristotle believed athletics had a deeper spiritual basis and taught good values for living. The ascetic discipline of Greek athletes became a model for the ascetic self-control used by Christian monks in the Middle Ages.

You can see the parallels yourself. Both athletic and spiritual disciplines

- Incorporate deep commitment and a willingness to stay focused
- Tap into virtues of fortitude, courage, perseverance, enthusiasm, and honor
- Enable participants to endure discomfort, even occasional pain, in order to awaken something within
- Create for some an illumination—called either a mystical moment of grace or "playing in the Zone."

Both may rouse people to a shared cause and bring them together in approved meeting places—churches, temples, mosques, stadiums, playing fields. Sometimes there's an overlap. Billy Graham's evangelical crusades and visits by the Pope draw so many people they often take place in sports stadiums.

Even when physical activity is practiced alone in no particular place, it often creates, by its very nature, a sacred time and space, just as the practice of prayer does. This seems especially true of outdoor activities. In a book about mountain climbing, Robert Schulteis wrote, "There is something about high places, something about lonely wild places in general—desert, sea, barren ground, the great salt lake—" He observed that such environments reach us in the wild place within our souls, the awesome inner depth where we meet God.

how to use this book . . . .

In thinking about a book that explores the connection between the physical and the spiritual, I wanted to learn from others. So you'll read forty-eight inspiring true stories about people who are physically active and whose activities helped them tap into a spiritual dimension. With few exceptions, these are not stories about professional athletes, but about ordinary men and women who simply love a particular sport or exercise.

You'll meet a North Carolina skydiver. A California surfer. A New Mexico hiker. A Massachusetts walker. The people I talked to range in age from a twenty-two-year-old college football player to a ninety-two-year-old Tai Chi instructor. Their stories reflect a variety of faith backgrounds.

Because their stories caused me to reflect so deeply on the connections between "sweat and the sacred," you'll also find my personal *Coach's reflection* at the end of each story.

Inevitably, we are imprinted by our beginnings and I was raised Catholic, so I reflect a Christian heritage. But I have tried to write a book that will be useful and interesting to people of various faiths—or who practice no particular religious doctrine.

If you're like many people today, you know the benefits of physical fitness and you may yearn to connect more intimately with God. You're just not sure how to do it.

So after the stories and reflections, you'll find specific steps you can use.

Pages 173–175 contain a two-part set of questions to help you assess your current attitudes about physical and spiritual exercise.

Next, you'll find twenty-one inspiring ways you can combine physical and spiritual fitness in your own life.

Finally, I've listed resources that helped me write this book and might help you if you choose to explore them.

There's a brilliant interweaving between body and soul. A dynamic connection between sweat and the sacred. It's my prayerful hope that this book helps you integrate both into your life.

Barbara Bartocci

stories to inspire you

1
CENTERING YOURSELF

walking, walking, walking . . . .

"Walking is a way to find spiritual replenishment, and anyone in a high-stress career needs that," says motivational speaker Bonnie Dean. So every morning when she's not traveling, Bonnie gets up early, whistles for Charlie the dog, and sets out through the woods behind her house in Bellingham, Washington.

Bonnie started her professional life as a fitness trainer working half a year in San Diego and the other half in Hawaii. With her trademark humor, she says, "I taught at a Hawaiian summer camp for overprivileged kids." Life changed when she and her husband divorced. "He got to keep San Diego. I got to keep the dog." Bonnie moved up the coast and shifted to a career in sales, then into motivational speaking. For a long while, she stayed fit by running long distances and pedaling her mountain bike up some serious terrain with her second husband.

Then she fell off a wall and injured her leg, and the accident brought chronic sciatica nerve pain. To help cope, she gave up high heels. Now she wears tennis shoes everywhere. "Just call me the speaker with *sole*," she grins, tilting one shoe.

On stage, she still exudes energy that goes way beyond any pain in her leg. Off stage, though, pain is often a daily partner. Bonnie gave up running and bicycling. "I've survived enough trauma that I'm writing a book. I call it, *I Can't Believe I Haven't Been on Oprah!*" She's learned, though, that there are compensations when you walk instead of run.

"When I walk in our woods, the first thing I feel is my shoulders loosening, as if a weight has lifted. My

17

breathing rhythm changes. I look out for roots, but I look up, too, because I love to spot birds. Adjacent to our property is a waterfall near an old stone bridge that was built in the 1930s. So as I walk, I listen to the splashing water and the noises of wood creatures, and the twitter of birds.

"I'm not a church member, but in the woods I feel as if it's not my shoe sole—it's my *soul* that is touched by God. And I pray. Mostly, I pray, 'Show me the direction you want me to go, O Lord. Show me the way for *today*." Out among the trees, with her waterfall splashing, it's easy, Bonnie says, to listen for God's response.

On the other side of the continent, in a small Massachusetts town, Carol Pirog walks, too. Her daily three-mile walk takes her into a cemetery. Sometimes in the rain.

When she told me this, I thought, I understand taking walks in the woods, along the seashore, or up a mountain. But walking in a *cemetery*? In the *rain*?

"Not *always* in the rain," laughs Carol. But yes, she recommends a cemetery as a great place for a daily walk. It's peaceful. Calming. And reading tombstones is a good reminder that life is a gift, and all of us eventually give the gift back to God. "It's a wonderful way to center yourself. At the same time, when I read my grandparents' tombstones—both of them are buried in the cemetery I walk in—it reminds me of life's continuum. It keeps you in the wheel of history."

Wheel of history. I like that phrase. Carol's cemetery is next door to her Catholic church, and she often ends her walk with daily Mass. It wasn't always so. For years, Carol was a dropout Catholic. Inexplicably, she went deaf in one ear, and in struggling to deal with her deafness, found herself listening more to God's voice. "And I felt as if God called me back to the church." Now she's one of her parish's most involved volunteers.

Walking through the cemetery is what grounds her; receiving the eucharist at Mass is what lifts her. To Carol, it's a pretty balanced way to start her day.

COACH'S REFLECTION: Like Bonnie and Carol, I, too, love to walk. It's one of the most powerful ways to "meditate in motion." The beauty of it is in its simplicity. All you have to do is step outside your front door.

Researchers report that a brisk twenty-to-thirty minute walk can have the same calming effect as a mild tranquilizer. When slower walkers add deep breathing (about six breaths per minute) their sense of well being equals that of faster walkers. And even more powerful results occur if you combine your walk with a repetitive prayer, such as the Rosary or a yoga mantra, synchronized to your breathing.

I don't need research reports to prove what I've already experienced, and if you're a walker, you don't either. Meditative walking turns physical exercise into spiritual exercise. It's good for the body . . . and transforming for the soul.

eyeing the tennis ball . . . .

Three times a week, Terry Bauman escapes the stresses of her life by running onto a tennis court. As soon as she grabs her racket, she knows she can stop thinking about all the "shoulds and musts" that occupy so much of her busy day. For an hour of intense singles play, she concentrates on only three things: "Me, the racket, and the ball."

Terry didn't grow up playing sports. She took up tennis in her mid-twenties, in the wake of the Billie Jean King phenomenon. Billie Jean was the first female athlete to earn $100,000 in a season. In the 1970s, as women everywhere pushed for equal rights, Billie Jean's trailblazing efforts for women's equality in tennis motivated thousands of women to take up her sport.

When you learn any sport as an adult, you're seldom as good at it as if you started as a child. But competition was never Terry's goal. Tennis was something she did for herself, an enjoyable way to learn and grow and get better at something that worked her physically.

She liked the game's rhythm. Run to get in place. Stop and set up. Pull back your arm, and keep your eye on the ball. Now hit it! *Run, set up, hit. Run, set up, hit.* Whether she chose a forehand stroke or a backhand, played a net game or a ground game, the essential rhythm remained, and the mental focus it required gave her a stimulating sense of connecting her mind and body.

In the 1980s, when Terry decided to earn an MBA, she knew it would be tough. It meant balancing night classes with her commitment to her family and her fulltime job as a stock broker. With such a tight schedule and the stress it produced, tennis became her saving grace.

"In tennis, the key to good play is to keep your eye on the ball. Don't look at the opponent. Don't get distracted. Just watch the ball." When she tossed a ball to serve, Terry liked to tell herself, "Focus on the label. Try to read it as the ball comes down. Is it a Wilson 1? Or a Wilson 2?" The rest of her day, she carried the same reminder with her. "Keep my eye on the ball. Stay focused on what I have to do *right now*. Don't get distracted."

When the bullish stock market of the 1990s plunged, tennis helped again. "I'd run onto the court, muttering, "So! Union Carbide is down sixteen points? Well, take that!" and I'd whack the ball furiously. That three inch round ball became a target for all my frustrations. It was a safe way to vent my pent-up emotions. When I remind myself to stay focused on the ball in tennis, I'm also reminding myself to stay focused on what's truly important in life," she said.

COACH'S REFLECTION: For Terry, the rhythm, the focus, and the willingness to set aside other distractions carried a connection to the sacred. Tennis reminded Terry to keep her eye on the ball. She was practicing one of Stephen Covey's *Seven Habits of Highly Effective People:* "Do *first* things first." I might substitute *"Seek first His kingdom.* (With the comforting knowledge that the gospel admonition continues, ". . . *and all else will be given to you."*)

But I've learned it's not always easy to stay focused on what we *say* is first. I might claim to put my family and my spiritual life first. Then demands of work take over, leaving less time for family or for God.

It's easy to delude our selves. One way to check is to keep a log for three weeks. How are you spending your *time* and your *money*? Knowing this will give you a clearer view of your priorities. Are you keeping your eye on the ball that counts?

dancing with spirit. . . . .

Ron Zoglin is wiry—his body is wiry and his hair is wiry, haloing his head in dark Einstein-type curls. He talks in a fast, exuberant style, and even his eyes smile. We are meeting so I can ask him about Sufi dancing, which emerged from the mystical tradition of Islam and is usually known in this country as Dances of Universal Peace. But quickly I learn that Ron is just as enthusiastic about Celtic dances: Welsh, Irish, Scottish.

Dancing is Ron's way of creating a harmony of body, heart, mind, and spirit. "Ignore any one of the four, and you won't feel integrated. Something will be missing," he says.

Not that Ron ever paid much attention to his own body when he was younger.

For years, he was more interested in his mind. It's constantly in motion, absorbing knowledge and new ideas. Ron is an antiques dealer, and co-authored a book on antiques. He's traveled the world searching for beautiful art objects.

He's a spiritual searcher, too, and loves exploring diverse spiritual paths.

But he wasn't a jock in school. Didn't run or kick or climb or feel a need to do anything athletic. His body was simply what housed the rest of him.

Like a lot of us, though, when he turned forty, Ron began to notice how other people aged. And he noticed that people who took *care* of their bodies seemed to age better. Maybe, he decided, he should stop taking his body for granted.

So he sampled various fitness programs. "Pick *anything* and I probably tried it," he says. "Jogging. Pushups. Training machines. After three weeks I'd get bored and quit." Then a friend mentioned a Celtic dance at a nearby church.

Ron hadn't thought much about dancing—in grade school and high school, he was usually a head shorter than most of the girls. But as soon as he experienced Celtic dancing, he knew. "I had found my exercise!" he says

He started lessons in Irish jigs, Scottish celidhs, Welsh reels. He learned line and reel dancing. And, eventually, because of his continued interest in ways to express the spiritual, he tried Dances of Universal Peace, in which dancers gather in a circle to embody spiritual unity, praise and give thanks, and offer prayers through movement for peace, love, and harmony.

I ask him to describe what he experiences while dancing. He closes his eyes for a moment, then murmurs,

"First, there's the *breath*. When you dance you breathe in full, rich, deep breaths. It's as if a life force enters my body and it stays with me even after I quit dancing.

"I don't *think* about what I'm doing with my feet, they take on a magic of their own. But I do notice eyes because when you meet or twirl your partner and make eye contact, for that instant, you create a relationship. And you feed off each other's energy.

"I'm fully engaged when I dance. I'm in the moment, not thinking about anything else. First, because it's a mental challenge, especially if you're new to the steps. Deborah (his partner) and I screw up a lot, but the more seasoned dancers are very forgiving. Very willing to help."

In Celtic dancing, dancers go through a sequence of prescribed steps, which eventually bring them back to their original positions. At its highest level, it's athletic, graceful, and complex. After an hour and a half (the length of a typical dance), Ron is sweating.

His experience is different in Sufi, or Dances of Universal Peace, because the steps are not complex. Participation, not presentation, is the focus. Dancers center their attention on creating community while celebrating the underlying unity of all of Earth's spiritual traditions. Christian, Jewish, Hindu, Buddhist, Islamic, Native American—all traditions are incorporated and honored. Sometimes sacred chants in their native languages are added. Most are only four lines long and repeated many times, so learning them is easy.

Whether it's a Celtic folk dance or a Sufi dance of universal peace, says Ron, "When I dance, I feel my spirit flow." His eyes crinkle in a smile. "I feel whole— as if my mind, heart, soul, and body are now one; truly in harmony."

COACH'S REFLECTION: Have you ever been home alone, put on a music CD, and then blissfully danced around your living room—bending, twirling, twisting, leaping—expressing your self in a way you never would if you thought someone was watching? I have.

"Dance increases the experience of the divine, and in many traditions, has been as much a part of religious expression as music," wrote Janet Weeks in *Dance Magazine*. The Psalmist agrees. "Sing to the Lord a new song . . . praise him with dancing and make music to him with tambourine and harp" (Ps 149:3).

I wish we danced more in church worship. I'm going to use it more often in my own meditation. Maybe you'll experiment, too. Let's loosen our bodies, praise with our feet, and see if we experience the oneness—the harmony—that Ron describes.

pilates: core strength . . . .

Liv Berger learned about "Pilates" when she was pirouetting her way to a dance degree at the University of California in Irvine. Then it was often called "dancer's therapy" because it was so popular with dancers.

The exercises were invented by Joseph Pilates, a skinny German kid who worked hard to become a gymnast and body builder. He was interred in a British POW camp during World War I, and to pass the time, began developing ways to help wounded soldiers recondition their bodies. In the 1920s, he emigrated to the U.S. and began helping athletes and dancers to rehabilitate their bodies after injury.

Pilates focused his exercises on the body's center, the part that dancers call the *power house*. The muscles at your core—diaphragm, pelvis, lower back, and buttocks—require strength and flexibility. Pilates believed that if your center is weak, the rest of your body becomes unstable, and eventually, you collapse in on yourself. Problems then occur in the hips, knees, and lower back.

At first, after Liv graduated from UC, she thought of Pilates simply as beneficial exercises she had learned how to do. Her focus was on her boyfriend. When he moved to Chicago for graduate school, she went with him, figuring she would pursue a dance career there.

But, as she puts it now, "I quickly realized I wasn't willing to be a starving dancer." Instead she began teaching Pilates' exercises part-time in a fitness studio. Then she became its manager, and discovered she had excellent business skills.

When she and her boyfriend broke up, Liv felt very alone. Chicago's a big city and she didn't know many people. But just as Pilates had strengthened her body, the steps she took to live on her own helped her find an inner strength she didn't know she had.

She took little steps at first. She ate in nice restaurants by herself. She grew comfortable walking alone into a concert. Then she started thinking about owning her own business.

By the mid-1990s, Pilates had become so popular, the exercises were showing up in mainstream fitness centers, so the time seemed right to open her own Pilates studio. Liv started small, setting up shop in her apartment. Then she rented space in a gym. She encouraged her clients by quoting a basic tenet of Pilates: "Physical fitness is a requirement for happiness." Her clients believed her because they experienced it for themselves. As their bodies gained grace, agility, and strength, so did their spirits. By word of mouth, Liv's reputation spread, and soon she needed larger quarters. Now, in her 2500-foot studio, she employs six other Pilates instructors.

Many clients like group classes on the mat. Others prefer to work one-on-one with Liv using her Pilates exercise machines, especially the *Reformer*. An odd-looking horizontal contraption, the Reformer uses belts and pulleys to help users re-form their core muscles along the principles Pilates developed in the POW camp. Some of the exercises are simple; many are complex, which is why most students like to work one-on-one with a trainer.

Liv told me the story of a client she calls "Jane." When she came to Liv, Jane was in her early thirties, had two kids and was getting divorced. She was overweight and very self-conscious about her body, with knee problems and poor upper body strength. Three months of Pilates' mat exercises strengthened her enough that Liv suggested an exercise on the *Reformer* to build more upper body strength. "I think you're ready for it, Jane."

Jane nodded and carefully watched as Liv showed her two Pilates movements that involved pull-ups. "Now you try." But when Jane started to pull herself up, she burst into sobs. Heartbroken cries. Shaking her head, unable to speak, she ran from the gym to the bathroom. By the time Liv reached her, her sobs had subsided, but she was still hiccupy and snuffly, like a little girl.

"Jane, what is it?"

"I remembered," sniffled Jane. "I was chubby and uncoordinated. And when I couldn't do pull-ups and push-ups in gym class, my teacher made fun of me—

criticized me—in front of everyone. I hated her. I hated every one of those kids who laughed at me!"

"Oh Jane, I'm so sorry—"

But now Jane was shaking her head, and smiling—*smiling*—through her tears. "No, it's okay. I'm glad that memory came back. I need to face it. And, by God, this time I'm going to *do* those pull-ups! I'm going to do them and move on."

As she told me the story, Liv smiled, too. Jane *did* do the pull-ups. And later, push-ups. "She was like a different person afterward. It was more than physical. I saw it in the way she handled her divorce and her new life. She'd found a deep core strength she didn't know she had.

COACH'S REFLECTION: Pilates believed that if your center is weak, the rest of you is weak and becomes unstable. Eventually, you collapse in on yourself.

One of the gospel stories offers a great metaphor for this. Two houses were built, one on rock and one on sand. When storm and wind arose, the house built on sand quickly collapsed. The house with a strong rock core weathered the storm.

Prayer is one of the best exercises I know to strengthen your spiritual core. It doesn't require formal words or going to church. It can be an informal conversation with God or a silent meditation, and can accompany any physical activity. But just as with exercise, prayer is not something you do only when you feel like it. You need to do it regularly, even if part of your mind feels cluttered with laundry lists of other "stuff."

After twenty years of starting each day with prayer, I can truly say this: on the occasional days when I *don't* spend time with God in the morning, my day simply doesn't go as well. The same thing is true when I don't exercise.

Rev. Martin Luther King, Jr. and Mother Teresa both said that the busier they got, the more time they set aside to pray. They knew what they needed to stay strong at the core.

figure skating with God . . . .

When you're a forty-pound overweight Spokane, Washington firefighter, figure skating is not the sport you immediately think about as *your* sport. Figure skating is for lithe, slender people in short skirts or tights. But for Frank Hornby, the graceful dance of figure skating was not only a gift from God; it became a way to honor God.

Frank pulled on skates the first time because he'd kept a promise to take his three kids skating, and it was cold in the rink. He figured he'd stay warmer if he skated. And he liked it! He liked it so much that a few weeks later, he started lessons so he could learn to skate backwards. Then he discovered he could rent time at the rink—at a discount—if he went very early in the morning. Finally, he took a deep breath, pulled out his wallet, and bought his own skates—a major commitment. You can pick up hockey skates for $150, but Frank's figure skates cost $450.

For a long time, Frank hid his sports passion from his fellow firefighters. Sure enough, when one of them discovered what he was doing, they ribbed him, especially the ones who played ice hockey. "Hey, Frank, you out there skatin' with the girls again?" Then a few of them noticed that, by now, Frank skated better than they did. He no longer carried forty extra pounds on his big-boned frame. His turns were quick and precise, and secretly, a few firefighters began asking him for lessons.

Frank laughs as he thinks back. "I figured out pretty quick that all I had to do was change the terminology and I could make the turns I taught 'em sound plenty macho."

For a long time, Frank's life had revolved around the firehouse, his family and his church. Now he added skating. One of his sons liked figure skating, too, and it was fun to skate together.

Then life skidded out of control. Frank retired as a firefighter, and his wife said she wanted a divorce. He was devastated. For a time, he slid into what he calls his "Eeyore mode," like the donkey in Winnie the Pooh, continually sighing, "Woe is me. Poor me."

The ice rink became his sanctuary, a place to go and feel sorry for himself. Then one day his skates hit a rough patch. His feet shot out from under him. As he fell to the ice, it was ". . . as if God was giving me a push and saying, 'Get up, Frank. Get going! You still have a lot to offer." He pulled himself up. The music started. He glided, twirled, and all of a sudden, a burst of joy filled him. "Life's not over!" he realized. As he continued to skate, he prayed: "Lead me, O Lord. Show me the way."

After that, he treated the ice rink as *God's* sanctuary, and skating became the gift he gave to God. He began working at an ice rink and started competing for amateur titles. In five years, he won four major medals. And although he still misses his marriage, he believes God is preparing him for what's coming next.

He has come to believe that life unfolds as it does for a reason. After all, he says, "I never planned on getting divorced, but I never planned on becoming a competitive figure skater, either. If you keep the faith, eventually you learn what God's plan is."

COACH'S REFLECTION: Frank's story made me think about the times when I, too, fell into "Eeyore mode." Sometimes resentment seemed stuck to me with Super Glue.

Then it's not easy to trust that God is at work, despite the outward circumstances of your life. "But the handiwork of the Creator can teach us if we will but listen," writes Richard Foster, in *The Celebration of Discipline.*

Frank's entry into competitive skating only occurred after he accepted the changes in his life. I had my own version of Frank's fall on the ice, and it woke me to some truths I needed to see, especially the important one of *letting go and moving on.*

Change also brings opportunity. Follow the advice of most athletic coaches: Put your losses behind you, make the most of what is, and get on with life. (The same lesson occurs in the gospel statement, "Shake the dust from your feet. . . .")

water laps . . . .

It's hard to get up at 6 a.m. when January Midwest temperatures dip below freezing. I have to push myself to leave my bed, pull on my swimsuit, and, shivering a little, my sweat suit. Downstairs, I grab jacket, hat, gloves. No garage so I need a few minutes to let my car warm up. It's still dark when I point my headlights toward the Athletic Club.

As I walk in the club's front door, another woman walks out, exercise bag in hand, dressed for work. *What time did she get up?* I wonder, impressed that she's already finished. Once inside, I hear the jazzy sounds of an early aerobics class, but my goal is the Olympic size lap pool, nestled for winter beneath a huge white plastic bubble. Often, this early, I'll be the only one in the pool, and in the solitude, it's easy to add prayer to my exercise.

There's a certain smell to an indoor pool. A humid, vinegary smell of chlorine mostly, different from the tennis shoe smell of a gym. Lights bounce off corner poles, and underwater lights reflect through the water. Since it's a lap pool, it's divided into four lanes, and never gets deeper than five feet. The heater makes a pulsing sound.

I drop a kick board and water-weights at the pool's edge, and climb down the ladder, splashing water on my wrists. Okay, not too cold. The pool is heated to eighty degrees in winter. I plunge underwater, pop up, hair streaming, and start taking long strides toward the pool's other end, spewing bubbles around me as I start to walk.

Before swimming, I like to walk in the water, partly as a physical warm-up, partly as a spiritual warm-up. I pray in time with my steps. For me, it's often a brief, mantra prayer that reflects my Christian tradition: *"Jesus, mercy. Christ, have mercy."* But any words can be used. It's the repetitive quality that quiets the mind and soothes the spirit. My prayer is background for my thoughts, which jump about as thoughts often do, but eventually may focus on a problem, an important relationship, or simple gratitude. *Thank you for a healthy body that allows me to swim.*

After twenty minutes of walking, I'm ready to go horizontal. I start with the kickboard. Up, back. Stop. Rest against the pool's edge. Breathe in slowly, deeply, three times. Recite: *"Calm mind."* Breathe out: *"Calm body."* My right arm lifts in the Australian crawl. Now left. I don't wear goggles, so I open my eyes underwater, making sure I swim above the center line. When I don't open my eyes, I tend to veer—wham!—into the side of the pool. As I reach the other end, I turn. Pause. Breathe slowly three times. *"Calm mind. Calm body."* Start back.

Every third lap, I flip and do the backstroke. My eyes trace the brown Rorschach-like weather-stains on the white plastic canopy as I extend each arm back, stretching my ribcage. A decorative line of nautical flags alert me when I'm six strokes from pool's end.

Back and forth, back and forth I swim, praying with each stroke until my hour is up. "Water," wrote Antoine de Saint-Exupery, "is not necessary to life, but rather *is* life itself. It fills us with a gratification that exceeds the delight of the senses." As I towel off and prepare to go about my day, I know just what he meant.

COACH'S REFLECTION: I've always loved the water, and took my first swimming lesson when I was five. My swimming teacher told me to let go of the edge, promising, "The water will hold you up." So I let go and promptly sank, like a small, round stone, coming up sputtering and scared. For a long while after that, I clutched the side of the pool as if my fingers were glued to its concrete edge. Yet once I learned to stop fighting and surrendered to the water, my body's natural buoyancy held me up beautifully.

I remembered that lesson as I sat in church recently. The pastor said, "There is a major difference between saying, 'I trust that if I let go, God will be there for me,' and the actual *act* of letting go, in absolute faith that God will be there."

How true, I thought.

Do you have faith that God's strengthening love will be there if you let go of something you're holding onto? It could be a job that no longer fulfills you. Resentment toward someone who hurt you. Or your own pride that keeps you from admitting you need help. What will it take to persuade you to release—in faith—the edge of your pool?

the paradox of yoga. . . . .

Tom Jacobs likes to end the yoga classes he teaches by having his students lay in a circle on their mats while he dims the lights. Then Tom, too, lies down, and as music plays softly behind him, he speaks quietly for several minutes about the connection between yoga and the rest of life. One of his students, with tongue in check, dubbed these talks, "Sermons on the Mat."

Tom laughs when he tells me that. He's a man with an easy laugh, a supple body, (especially for someone nearing fifty), and a short ring of dark hair surrounding a clean-shaven head. His eyes crinkle in smile lines. He teaches yoga six nights a week, and to him, it's "Prayer of the body."

Not that he immediately announces that idea to new students. "Most people come to my classes the first time because they're on the edge of burnout," he says. "All kinds of people—mothers, nurses, lawyers, doctors. They're seekers, looking for relaxation, flexibility, and often, deeper meaning to their lives.

"I try to de-mystify yoga and talk about it in a down-to-earth way. Soon enough, I know they'll experience for themselves the peace within chaos that is so much a part of *doing* yoga."

The word *yoga* means union, and for Tom, that's what life is about: finding union with God, whatever way that union expresses itself to individuals. As the son of a Jewish father and a Catholic mother, he early accepted the idea that God is larger than any one doctrine.

"My soul was always intrigued with the sheer *mystery* of God, so I wanted to be part of communities where others were pursuing the same mystery. I wanted to sit in communal meditation and start each day with a conscious awareness of Divine Presence," says Tom. He spent four years as a Catholic Benedictine monk and another five years living as a community member in a Catholic retreat center.

Another community member practiced yoga regularly, and Tom was so captivated by the gracefulness and beauty of *asanas* (yoga positions) that he asked to study with him.

"It was a time in my life when I was working through a number of issues, and wondering in what direction I was meant to go. Certain Yoga positions gave me an extraordinary emotional release," he recalls.

He was experiencing what he now tells students is the paradox of yoga: finding peace amidst pain; and calm amidst chaos. Yoga is about more than creating a flexible body. As Tom puts it, "It can make you peaceful in other parts of your life, from navigating rush hour traffic to dealing with money issues to your personal relationships."

Tom shows beginners the basic Mountain Pose where you stand with arms at your sides, experiencing the stillness and stability associated with mountains. He illustrates the extended Triangle where the body forms a triangle and one arm lifts high to the sun. He reminds students, "Yoga isn't a competitive sport. Honor *your* edge. Don't compare to someone else's flexibility. If the person next to you touches her toes and you can only touch your knees, it's okay. That's your edge right now. Do what works for you. And remember to breathe."

Breath, says Tom, is one of the strongest doorways to God. It's a way to experience your union with God. Breath is free. It is unconditional. It is inside you and all around you. It sustains you. Just as God sustains you. Whether you call it Divine Energy, Prana, or Grace, it means the same, and yoga helps you release its flow through your body. Yoga is a foundation for bringing you closer to God.

In addition to leading yoga classes, Tom makes his living by leading meditation workshops and performing as a singer and songwriter of music praising God. Stretching, breathing, meditating, singing—they are all one to him. All part of a ministry in which he encourages others to find and experience their unity with God. To Tom, it's what life is all about.

COACH'S REFLECTION: After knee surgery, I knew I needed to make stretching a regular part of my life. I turned to yoga, relishing the way my spine and lower back, knees and legs seemed to lengthen and grow stronger. With a yoga instructor like Tom Jacobs, there's also a stretching of the soul.

In thinking about my soul, I remember something I heard years ago. Inside each of us there is a God-shaped hole. Problems emerge when we try to fill the hole with nothing more than worldly things—such as money, titles, or maybe a Porsche. We can't understand why we feel dissatisfied. But it's because we haven't filled the hole. The hole is shaped so only God can fill it.

If you feel an odd emptiness inside, maybe it's time to ask: "Am I practicing the breath of Life? Do I start each day by getting in touch with the Divine Presence? Am I trying to fill my God-shaped hole with other stuff?" And then, "Is it time to sign up for a yoga class?"

canoeing with clarity...........

In 1995, Dr. Ian Ritchie's mind was filled with plans. He was driving to Winnipeg, Canada from Montreal to start a new job teaching religion and culture at Concord College. The truck he drove held everything he owned, including his precious canoe.

Driving north along the shore of Lake Superior, Ian reached Pancake Bay Provincial Park. He'd been there several times as a boy, and the sparkling bay held good memories. It was a beautiful spot to camp that night. And perfect for canoeing!

As a theologian, Ian had presented scholarly papers with such heavy titles as "Humanity and Nature in African Traditional Religions," and "Sensory Ratios in the Hebrew Bible." But another side of him was that of a simple outdoorsman who loved wilderness hiking, and who had canoed most of his life. The tranquil solitude of canoeing was close to a religious experience.

Eagerly, he untied his canoe and put it in the water. Drifting clouds made shadows on the water. High above, two hawks circled. A slight breeze, tinged with pine, stirred his hair. As he paddled out from shore, he noticed how clean and pure the water was. It was quiet, with the peculiar silence of the natural world.

He propelled his canoe smoothly, filling his lungs with the fresh, clean air. And as he paddled, he thought about the rhythms of life. Ten years earlier, he'd been preparing to leave Nigeria in West Africa, after five years of working with a Mennonite relief agency. Last year, he had been a college chaplain. Soon he would be teaching again. Where will I be in another ten years? He wondered.

But trying to foresee the future was like looking at the sun; all that was visible was amorphous light. The water, on the other hand, was so clear it was like looking through crystal. He could see twenty feet down to the ridges of sand on the bottom.

As he watched the sand shift and move, he felt intensely present to the moment. He saw the shadow of his canoe, with him in it, on the bottom of the lake, and he felt as if he were in the world, but suddenly it was the world made more real than usual. He felt a powerful connection with the infinite. A sense of being linked to the water, the sand, the sky, the air, and all related somehow to God.

In that moment, said Ian later, he felt God's presence in a way he never had before, despite all his studies *about* God and *about* theories of religion. The power of that mystical experience never left him.

Today he seldom writes a heavy religious treatise. He does pastoral work as an assistant curate, and his homilies, which often appear on the Web, have such popular titles as "Trusting God When It Hurts," and "Finding the Sacred Place." Although several other events helped in his decision to change his life's direction, Ian traces part of the shift to his incredible afternoon of canoeing on Pancake Bay. Where the mystical presence of God and the very world itself became, for a moment, more real than real.

COACH'S REFLECTION: In my own life, I've learned that one of the great benefits of outdoor activity is the opportunity to "get away from it all." It truly can lead you to a glimpse of the infinite. In his sermon on sacred places, Dr. Ritchie himself said it this way:

centering yourself

"Real solitude has a rare and deep quality to it, where the purity of aloneness is truly healing, partly because it has been sought out rather than imposed. Going on a wilderness journey can bring a deeper experience of God's presence."

In solitude lies the opportunity to awaken to life's deepest questions: "Who am I?" "Why am I here?" "What is my life about?" And you may find, as Ian did, a rare moment of clarity—when the water is crystal clear, your eyes see, and your heart responds.

2
OVERCOMING FEAR

black diamond skier. . . . .

When I signed up for a women's ski seminar in Aspen, Colorado, I did it in that limbo period between separating from a spouse and signing final divorce papers. It was a difficult time—our marriage had lasted twenty years before burning out—and the ski seminar offered a way of proving something to myself, though I wasn't sure what.

I gathered with four other women at the top of Aspen Mountain. Sandy from LA, in a bright yellow jumpsuit, raised her ski pole exuberantly. "I hope we tackle some tough runs!" she exclaimed. I gulped and responded, "Look, I'm strictly intermediate. I don't ski black diamond runs."

"Not to worry," said a reassuring voice, and we turned to meet Trish, our red-haired ski instructor. "This is an intermediate class."

We started by skiing past a video camera, the snow crunching like popcorn popping. Later, as we watched tapes, Trish urged, "Find something you like about your skiing." I tried, but all I saw was my fanny sticking out and my arms flailing like windmills.

Still, we murmured encouragement to each other, and as the day progressed, so did we. Pat managed to ski baby moguls without falling. Rosanne improved her turns. Sandy showed real grace as she hurtled down a slope. Snow showered from our skis as we followed Trish down one run after another like so many obedient ducklings.

Then came a run that dropped more precipitously than any other we'd skied. "Just remember to crouch," said Trish, "and follow me." She pushed off so quickly that no one had time to think. Our poles flicked the snow as we slid down after her. *Crouch, turn! Crouch, turn!* Down, down, until—"I did it!" I cried.

Trish beamed. "Yes, and you just skied a black diamond run."

My grin could have lit up New York. "A black diamond?" Suddenly I felt like that old Helen Reddy song of the 1970s. "I am invincible. I am Woman!"

But then Trish headed for another black diamond run. The first had been steep but wide; this was a narrow chute with trees on one side and a sheer drop on the other.

"I—I can't do it," I stammered.

"Sure you can. Two turns, maybe three, and you'll be down," said Trish as she slid over the edge. The others followed. I stayed frozen at the top. Finally, Trish called, "Sidestep it Barb." And ignominiously, I half-stepped, half-fell down the slope.

The group made comforting noises. "We all freak out on something." "Don't give up." And from Trish, "You may see the run differently another day. Remember, it's simply a matter of up here." She tapped her head. "Don't let fear hold you back. At a certain point you have to let go and trust."

In the remaining two days of my ski vacation, I stayed on the safe blue slopes and worked on technique. On my last afternoon, though, something drew me to the run that had freaked me out. I peered down the chute. My stomach curdled. The trees rose like a fir barrier. The cliff dropped off into nothingness. "I don't ski black diamonds," I said. I whispered it, ghostlike, an echo of all my old beliefs. "I don't do divorce either," I added. But here it was in my life.

Abruptly, I hurled myself forward. Shrieking in fear—"I'm going to crash! Turn! The cliff! I'm going over the cliff! Turn! Crouch, turn!" I spraddled into an awkward snowplow position like a drunken duck. But Trish was right. Three turns and I'd made it.

I caught my breath and looked back up the run—the narrow ledge, the plunging edge. The air crystallized in my lungs. Then I smiled.

I'd gone over the precipice and survived. I hadn't done it gracefully, but I'd done it. If I could get down a black diamond ski run, surely I could maneuver my way through divorce. I just had to trust—and allow myself more than one run.

COACH'S REFLECTION: Faith in God and our own higher selves doesn't mean a problem-free life. I've learned it means responding to new challenges whenever and however they appear, believing that we have the strength within to overcome our fear, and to jump right over life's precipices.

Whether it's skiing a scary slope, mastering a sailboat in a storm, or running farther than you thought you could, mastering a physical challenge helps in the mastery of other challenges.

The unknown medieval author of *The Imitation of Christ*, put it this way: "When adversity comes, if like strong and mighty champions, we would fight strongly, we should undoubtedly see the help of God come in our need."

Yes. Hold the image of yourself as a champion. Even if you feel like an awkward duck.

grace in gale winds . . . .

My parents, when they lived in southern California, owned a cabin cruiser, but I had never much cared for it. The engine was noisy, and we bumped across waves—*Thump! Thump! Thump!*—as if the boat had hiccups. The speed tousled my hair and the wind made it hard to hear. A motorboat to me was like a bus, just a way to get to where you wanted to go.

Then a friend invited me to go sailing on his thirty-foot sailboat—and oh, what a difference. The sail blossomed against the sky like a lily. All was quiet, so quiet that as I gazed about, everything seemed part of one whole: the boat, the water, the sail, the wind, all working together. Immediately I sensed a spiritual connection, because in sailing, it's not about getting there: it's about the joy of the journey.

I was a passenger that day. Other, more experienced crew were aboard who knew what to do when my friend called "Ready about?" and who grabbed a line as the sailboat slowly turned. The most I learned to do was avoid the boom when it swung over.

Not so Karen Hawkins, a designer of trade show exhibits that I recently met. With her sun-lightened hair, well-defined arms, and self-confident air, I could easily picture her at a sailboat's tiller. She had learned to sail as "a little kid," she told me, and took advanced sailing lessons as a teen.

In her twenties, she made a dream come true. She agreed to crew aboard a forty-six-foot cutter that was sailing from Bermuda to New York. "So many people yearn to sail the Atlantic, and set aside their dreams because they think they need to find more 'practical' work. I didn't want that to happen to me," she said, with the experience of a woman in her forties.

I asked if sailing gave her a feeling of spiritually connecting. She circled the air with one arm. "Everything is connected. It's all one. What I've learned from sailing is how small I am—*and* how large I am."

She described in vivid detail the night she felt small. She and two others were halfway to New York from Bermuda. The crew of three—Karen, the boat's British owner, and another sign-on from Florida—had sailed through several uneventful, sunlit days. Then, a little after dusk one evening, a storm rose. At seven mph, the maximum speed for a sailboat, you can't outrun a storm. You hope for early weather reports so you can steer perpendicular to the wind and avoid the worst of it. But information had reached them too late.

As winds picked up, the water turned choppy. The sail rig started shuddering. Karen and the others ran to close hatches, take down sails, turn on the motors, and fasten themselves to the boat with lines.

Winds grew fiercer. The air was supercharged with noise. Waves, cresting now at fifteen feet, threw the boat up, then *slammed* it down. "It felt as if a telephone pole was hitting the hull like a baseball bat!" said Karen. As waves tossed the boat, the red and green starboard and port lights reflected off a *wall* of water. "We could only strap in and go along for the ride. If one of us got washed overboard, at least we were tethered to the boat, although sailors have died in harnesses, too." She prayed that night, not so much in words, but with an inarticulate sense of holding onto God as tightly as she gripped her tether.

The terrifying gale lasted two hours, and winds were clocked at fifty-seven mph. "The storm taught me just how small and inconsequential I am," said Karen.

But there was a paradox. Sailing also made her feel larger. It stretched her. "To me, spiritual growth is all about learning to know yourself. And you can't know yourself unless you take some risks. Sailing helped me grow comfortable with risk. It helped me believe in my own abilities." She paused. "Sailing is so much more than a journey over water."

I remembered my own small epiphany—that moment of instant knowing on my friend's boat, when I realized that sailing is not just about getting there; it's all about the joy of the journey. I might never be the sailor that Karen is, but I understood exactly what she meant.

COACH'S REFLECTION: *"Then the Lord spoke to Job out of the storm."* When our lives feel most perilous is often the time that we hear God speak. And the word of God may not be perceived in words, but in some inarticulate knowledge that we are small and lost, but have something larger than ourselves to cling to.

Karen told me that a few days after the storm, she relaxed on the sailboat's deck, enjoying the sun, sky and now-gentle waves. She pulled in several very deep breaths—filling her lungs, absorbing the sea air into her body. "And ever since," she said, "any time I need it, I feel as if the ocean's breath is still inside me, as part of my core, and it strengthens me."

Take a moment to breathe deeply, whether you're on a boat, walking along a beach, or sitting in a lawn chair. Can you feel in your breath the living spirit, inspiring and strengthening you?

martial arts and courage . . . .

Susan Longenecker learned many things from practicing martial arts, but perhaps the most significant is summed up in this line: *Feel the fear and do it anyway.*

In the late-1970s, Susan was a twenty-something marine biologist, happy in her job with the Environmental Protection Agency in Florida. One day, as she and her boyfriend drove across one of the Florida causeways, they saw a pick-up truck veering erratically as it hurtled across the bridge.

"Drunken idiot!" muttered her boyfriend. He pulled his van off the road to let the drunk go by, but instead, the pick-up, as if magnetized, came directly at them.

"Oh my God—" and then mercifully, Susan blacked out. She doesn't remember the horrendous crash that killed the drunk, put her boyfriend in a coma for two weeks, and sent her head crashing into the side window as her foot twisted and smashed through the van's console. She came to as they were being airlifted to a nearby hospital.

Susan's injuries healed, with the help of a steel plate in her neck, but her pain lingered. Desperate for some relief, she followed a doctor's suggestion to try exercise, and signed up for a karate class. "I knew nothing about martial arts," she told me as we talked twenty years later. "I had never played sports as a kid and I wasn't very coordinated." But she was willing to try anything to ease her discomfort.

Donning the stiff white uniform of a student, Susan learned to bow to her *sensei* (instructor) in a traditional gesture of respect and do *katas* (a basic set of choreographed moves) with a partner. When she practiced karate, she forgot her pain, and soon began going to sessions four times a week, two hours at a time.

Susan's hard work paid off as she earned progressive colored belts. But one aspect of karate frightened her: combat with an opponent, even if the moves were designed for self-defense. Ironically, she wasn't afraid of being hurt, but of hurting someone else.

"I was raised in that transitional generation of women, and my mother's messages to me as a child still echoed. 'Susan, be nice.' 'Don't hurt anyone.' Mom meant don't hurt someone's feelings. She would have been horrified to think I could hurt someone physically. But in physical contact, if you lose control, it will happen. That's what scared me—that I would lose control."

Whenever she was called to engage in contact, her fear erupted all over again. Once, hoping her instructor would let her off, she cried, "Oh, I'm going to throw up!" Without a pause, he replied, "Very well, do it and get it over with. Then go to the mat."

"Every single time I had to go to the mat, I felt sweaty and scared," says Susan. "Every single time, I had to take a deep breath and re-conquer my fear."

So, did it happen? *Did* she ever hurt someone?

Susan sighed. Nodded. "I can still hear the awful *crack* as his nose broke."

She was an advanced belt by then and practicing with another instructor. As planned, she reached up, grabbed his ears, yanked him forward, and drove her knee toward his face. During practice, she was supposed to pull back before contact; but Susan was tired, and once in motion, her knee kept going. It was her worst nightmare come true.

But karate trains students to release their failures as well as their fears. Her instructor sent Susan back to the mat. Gradually, as she continued to practice and face her fears, she gained more self-control. And more confidence that she could stay in control. One day she realized, "It's true! Whatever frightens you—if you face it—*will* pass."

COACH'S REFLECTION: One of the greatest benefits of physical activity is the way it pulls us out of our comfort zones. You discover, "I *did* it! I conquered my fear and did it! And if I can do this, why, I can do *that* (whatever your personal *that* might be)."

Every major religion offers admonitions against fear. In Deuteronomy, "Do not be faint-hearted and afraid. . . for the Lord your God goes with you." In Christian gospels, "Do not be afraid for I am with you."

In my own life, I've learned that courage is not the absence of fear but the *mastery* of it, and mastery comes only after you step out, even if it's with fear and trembling.

Ask yourself if fear has kept you from tapping into your own greatest potential. Then accept that you're afraid, but instead of letting fear hold you back, step out anyway. Think of it as lifting weights, and start small by taking small risks, building up to larger ones. As Susan learned, "Whatever frightens you *will* pass."

the running nun . . . .

Headphones are a desecration, says Laverne Aufmuth. Laverne is a runner in my home town. She's also a nun, and when she runs, it's her time for meditation, for silently praising God, and, perhaps most of all, for *listening* to God.

Sr. Laverne is one of many "professional religious" who love to run. For them, body and soul are meant to go together. By using their bodies and strengthening them, they feel they are deepening the grace in their souls.

Probably the most famous running nun is Sr. Marion Irvine from California. In 1983, at age fifty-four, she ran the California International Marathon in 2:51:01, which qualified her for the 1984 Olympic trials. She was the oldest American runner in that marathon to qualify for the trials. Immediately the media dubbed her "The Flying Nun."

Running a marathon was not Sr. Laverne's goal. Staying alive was. When she joined her religious community in the late 1950s, girls didn't play sports, nuns still wore long habits, and females in the Church obediently did whatever they were told. After the Vatican II Council in 1962, Sr. Laverne, and other nuns, too, became more independent. She moved from a convent to an apartment, went from traditional habit to modern dress, and returned to school to become a registered nurse.

It was an exhilarating but stressful time. When both her parents died of heart-related problems. Laverne felt overwhelmed. Did her parents' early deaths put her at risk, too? She decided to start running as a way to relieve stress. "Running fit my schedule and my budget. I could go out early in the morning, and all I needed was a pair of shoes."

She didn't know what she was doing. Didn't know about proper stretching or the possibility of shin-splints. Didn't understand the importance of cooldowns or what pounding a pavement could do to knees. She simply began: a slow jog at first for less than a mile. Gradually, she increased her distance until she was running two miles most mornings. The physical-ness of it—the pumping of her arms, stretching of her thighs, even her gasps for air when she went up a long hill—invigorated her. It gave her a new perspective on endurance and pain. She noticed, in a more celebratory way, the beauty of God's creation—the greening trees, freshly barbered grass, a rabbit hunched in quivering anticipation, the sweet perfume of lilacs.

For several years, running was a solitary sport for Laverne. Then she started running in a popular city park, and one morning, noticed two women running ahead of her. When they stopped, Laverne caught up with them. Before long they had formed a runner's club.

Running with friends is different from running alone, yet for Sr. Laverne, it's still a mix of physical and spiritual. "I see God's presence in everyone I run with. I look at each as a blessing."

No, she's not the flying nun. She still hasn't run a marathon, and probably never will. With a slight twinkle, she says, "God helps me stay humble by showing me what I can do and what I can't do." But running strengthened her, and became, for her, another way to connect with God. And perhaps it helped her become a better instrument of God.

COACH'S REFLECTION: I have always loved these words from Isaiah: *"Hope in the Lord and you will be strengthened. . . you will run and not grow weary."* Sr. Laverne started running as a way to deal with stress. Most of us would agree with her: Life does seem unusually stressful today. I hear so many people worrying about terrorism, war, disease, or financial uncertainty. Yet when has life *not* been marked by stress, either personal or global?

Tranquility depends, not on peace in the world, but on the peace we carry within. Exercise helps us handle stress better by increasing the endorphins in our brains. But the key to a truly serene spirit comes from placing our "hope in the Lord." In knowing there is a powerful Reality beyond the visible world we see. It's this power that gives us strength to run and not grow weary. (But I still have to remind myself, it helps to take *off* the headphones.)

wrestling coach. . . . .

At forty-six, Ron Leugers is still built like a wrestler: short, stocky, muscular. He's blonde, in good shape and looks younger than his years. Today he's wrestling with a very different set of circumstances from those he experienced as a high school wrestler and during his career as an Air Force non-commissioned officer.

Many people, says Ron, confuse the sport of wrestling with the fake matches seen on cable TV. The real sport is a disciplined practice demanding physical endurance, a carefully honed body, speed, strength, and agility.

Ron wrestled his first match in sixth grade. His opponent had him on the mat in seconds, but Ron liked the sport, and as soon as he reached high school, he tried out for the team. Their coach was demanding. At their first practice, he yelled, "Drop!" In unison, thirteen members of the wrestling team dropped to the floor for 400 push-ups. Then 400 sit-ups. Followed by jumping jacks. Weight lifting. Exercises to strengthen their necks. By the end of practice, Ron was sweating and sore. But his coach cut no slack. "Come on, you guys. Don't quit. Try again. Put out the effort."

He required a lot, but he also gave Ron a lot of encouragement, and Ron soaked it up like a dry sponge tossed into water. It was so different from what he heard at home where his mother had been divorced several times and his alcoholic stepdad was often abusive.

Ron worked hard to learn the wrestling throws. *Take down. Spin. Escape.* He showed up every day for three-hour workouts. And soon his coach saw something in Ron that Ron didn't see in himself. "Put out the effort, boy. *Practice.* You can do it. Don't let any struggle or defeat keep you down. Get up off the mat. Try again. You can do it!"

His words pushed Ron. At weekend tournaments, where each match was a tough, one-on-one, six-minute contest, Ron was a strong competitor. He showed speed, endurance, and a great sense of timing. By his senior year, he was ranked third in the state of Ohio.

"My coach invested in me," says Ron, looking back. "Thanks to him, I learned how to think like a champion." He had learned to believe in himself and recognize his own abilities. When he joined the Air Force, he liked the military structure. It provided boundaries and rules, something he was used to in sports. He continued to wrestle in service competitions, and moved up quickly to become a top NCO.

One day, a service buddy invited Ron to go with him to a church service, which began Ron's quest for a deeper relationship with God. His Christian faith remains a core part of his life today.

Ron joined a trucking company after he left the Air Force and was promoted into senior management. Life seemed good, especially after he and his wife Colette had their first baby.

But last year, the trucking company went bankrupt, leaving Ron and 15,000 other employees without jobs. Now Ron is starting over near the bottom.

He isn't discouraged. "Every life has its victories and defeats, but I have faith, and that means I'm expected to hang in there. If you stay faithful, you don't quit, and you keeping giving of yourself—110 percent."

I suggested that those appeared to be the same lessons he learned from his high school wrestling coach. Ron flashed an easy smile and tapped his Bible. "I'm lucky," he said. "I had more than one coach."

COACH'S REFLECTION: What is a coach but someone who shows you the way to perform at your very best? More than one Christian athlete has called Jesus "the great coach" but believers of every faith have their "great coaches." When you run into difficulty, ask yourself these three questions:

① Who has been your coach in the game of life?

② What have you learned?

③ How can those lessons help you in the situation you face now?

hiking high places . . . .

Hiking in the mountains is an incredible adventure because it puts you in touch with nature at its grandest. But I have an almost phobic reaction to "ledges with edges"—those narrow paths that have a sheer drop-off on one side.

I wasn't thinking about narrow ledges, though, on the sunny October day when my friend Jane and I started up a popular Colorado trail, headed for Cathedral Lake. I'd never been there but had heard it was beautiful.

Our trail wound through Aspen groves, shimmering gold, then alongside a rushing stream. Magpies flitted in trees. Gradually, the trail grew steeper, and I hunched forward.

We rounded a curve—and I gasped. Our trail had disappeared into a wide moraine of loose rocks—"scree" mountaineers call it. Boulders of all sizes, torn loose by some long ago avalanche, dotted the side of the mountain. To keep climbing we had to follow a series of narrow ledges that zigzagged through the scree as if some giant hand had carved the mark of Zorro. They were definitely ledges with edges.

Jane, who had hiked the trail before, said, "Don't worry. Once we climb through this, we'll be at the lake."

Not wanting to admit my fear, I followed Jane, gingerly picking my way through the loose rock. Except for the click of our boots against stone, there was only that peculiar crystal clear silence that is part of high altitudes.

Each switchback was just wide enough for me to place one foot after another. I concentrated on keeping my balance, trying not to look over the edge or think how easily I could slip and fall. We had reached the seventh turn when I stumbled. My foot slid and I grabbed frantically at empty air. "You're okay!" shouted Jane. Her fingers clutched mine and held tightly until I regained my balance. My lungs burned, not from exertion but from panic. I felt like someone trapped on the outside ledge of a skyscraper. "I'm afraid," I whispered.

"We're almost at the top," said Jane. "You can make it."

I hardly heard her. My mind was frozen on one sentence, repeating it over and over: "Don't move, don't move, don't move." Even bending my fingers frightened me, as if the slightest shift might send me plummeting. When a gust of wind tugged at my windbreaker, I whimpered. A pebble ricocheted down the mountain. It sounded like a gunshot.

Finally, I took a frightened step forward—only because two turns up seemed better than seven down—and sure enough, soon the trail widened, and

I could grab the comforting branch of a pine tree. We came into a wide, lush, alpine meadow. Scattered wildflowers could still be glimpsed and where there weren't flowers, tall, waving grass stirred like wheat. Cutting through the meadow was a stream that ended in a crystal clear lake.

We pulled peanut butter sandwiches and crisp apples from our backpacks, washing our food down with good, cold water from our canteens. Yet even as we laughed and clambered around the meadow, I felt a tug of fear. Eventually we had to start down again, and I would face those terrifying marks of Zorro.

The sky turned gray, precursor to an afternoon storm—a common event in the mountains—and as I thought about the narrow ledges, slippery with rain, my stomach turned queasy.

"We'd better start down," said Jane.

"I know."

At the switchbacks, Jane offered to go first and talk me down. I shook my head. I knew I needed more than Jane's cheery voice. Fear held me like a vise. I closed my eyes, and felt a prayer, inarticulate at first, just a few chaotic words: *Oh God, I'm so afraid. Help me.*

Abruptly, an odd image appeared in my mind. High in the mountains, I was picturing a boat. It was the familiar gospel story about Jesus' disciples, begging him to quiet a storm that threatened to drown them. Their fear was my fear. So into my mind, I brought a visual image of Jesus, stretching out his hand to me. I held out my own hand, and with my hand still out, as if grasped by comforting fingers, I began edging down the trail. As I walked, I talked, my words running together.

"Thank you for helping me down Jesus I know you're with me just as you were with your disciples you won't let me slip there made the first turn keep holding my hand thank you thank you here's the second turn. . . "

And so, step by anxious step, talking all the while, I inched my way down the nine zigzags.

"You did it!" crowed Jane.

I laughed giddily as I looked back up the steep slope. "I did, didn't' I? But I had some very special help."

COACH'S REFLECTION: It's been several years since that hike, but the visualization of Jesus holding my hand has never left me. Depending on your own religious outlook, you might have visualized a different guide: perhaps your guardian angel.

I think my experience is a good reminder that all of us possess more strength than we realize to manage life's inevitable zigzags. *"Be not afraid"* is a guiding precept of most religious faiths. The next time you feel caught up in fear, hold out your hand—as I still do, even today. Picture the warm clasp of your spiritual guide, be it the risen Lord or another revered figure. Or simply your own stronger self. Have faith that you can tap into the help you need to traverse any scary path you are on.

3
FINDING HEALING

karmic arrows . . . .

The first time Beth Erlichmann held a bow and arrow in her hands, she was seven. It was a child's toy, a gift from her great-uncle Walt who lived in Texas. The second time she picked up a bow was forty years later in Boston as she recovered from a mastectomy. Now it was not a toy, but a tool Beth hoped would help her heal.

Of all things, it was her oncologist who had suggested she try archery after her surgery. And not just any archery, but a Japanese form called *Kyudo*.

"Bending your bow will use the right muscles to help you physically," she said. "and just as important, it's very calming. A standing meditation, really. You're so absorbed in the process, it soothes you mentally. I learned about *Kyudo* from my yoga teacher."

Beth needed soothing. A mastectomy is hard on any woman. But she was newly single, after a long, troubled marriage. What would it be like, she wondered, to try and date again? Would anyone want a woman with one breast?

So she joined four other *Kyudo* students in a gymnasium. They faced a straw target. Their instructor wore a traditional white keiko-gi (kimono) and a black, floor-length hakama, or divided skirt.

"*Kyudo* is not about hitting the target," he said. "*Kyudo* is about finding your spirit. If your spirit is weak, your shooting will be lifeless. When the spirit is strong, you're like a deep-flowing river. Calm on the surface but with tremendous power underneath."

He showed them the eight stages of shooting. When done right, he explained, they became a continuous, flowing sequence all the way through *Kai*. *Kai* was when the arrow released. As it left the bow, the archer held position and sent forth his or her spirit to accompany the arrow.

One of the more experienced students whispered, "Sometimes we only shoot two arrows in a half hour. It's all about the sequence of movements. Not about hitting the target."

Beth did her best to follow instructions.

Keep your body erect. Spread your feet apart the distance of one arrow length.

Distribute weight evenly. Hold the fiberglass bow at hip level. (Original bows were bamboo).

Shoulders, hips, feet aligned. Spine gently stretched. Shoulders flat. Gaze at the target through calm, half-closed eyes, sending your spirit forward. Then, raise the bow perfectly straight, arrow parallel to the floor. Arms and chest relaxed.

"Don't focus on the shooting, but on the moment at hand," their instructor intoned. "You are seeking truth, goodness and beauty." Beth almost smiled, but he looked so serious, she immediately bit her lip.

Truth, she learned, meant shooting with the right intent, and with body and soul in harmony. Goodness meant courtesy, compassion, and non-aggression. Beauty meant grace and artistry, even down to small touches, like wearing well-pressed attire.

"Marksmanship is not important," said the instructor. "The goal is to polish the mind."

At first, Beth didn't get it. She planned to stay for the five introductory lessons because she had paid her fee and she'd promised her doctor. But archery that didn't care if you hit the target? What kind of sport was that?

Her doctor had told her she was lucky. She didn't need chemotherapy. But there were still eight weeks of radiation treatments after her mastectomy. And Beth hated it. She hated having to go every week. Hated it when the technician drew indelible lines on her chest with a magic marker. Hated having her body zapped with something she knew could burn her—and, one week, did.

Her *Kyudo* lessons continued during the same period as her outpatient radiation. And one afternoon in the gym, as she focused her attention on slowly lifting her bow, keeping feet and shoulders aligned, breathing in a relaxed fashion, picturing herself as a smoothly flowing river, she *did* get it. As she reached *Kai* and felt her arrow release, her body seemed to lighten, as if something in her spirit let go. She understood then that it *didn't* matter if her arrow hit the target. What mattered was the exquisite peace she felt in that moment. "All will be well," she murmured.

As Beth spoke to me later, describing her *Kyudo* experience, she said she understands why the meditative archery has traveled beyond Japan to find adherents in the U.S., Norway, Germany, Australia and beyond. "I'll bet you can even find *Kyudo* in west Texas where Uncle Walt lives," she says with a quick laugh.

She now owns her own hakama and keiko-gi, and practices at the gym three times a week, trying to make her movements as smooth as flowing water. The target is like a mirror, reflecting how she feels at the moment.

"*Kyudo* has helped me stand taller," says Beth. "I believe in myself more, and I'm at peace now with my body. If I meet someone, and he doesn't want me because of my mastectomy, well—" she shrugs, smiles. "In that case, I don't want him."

COACH'S REFLECTION: After talking to Beth, I went on the web to look up *Kyudo*. And there I read the comments of Swami Jnaneshvara Bharti, who refers to arrows as metaphors.

"Arrows in flight are actions and speech that are already playing themselves out in your life, and cannot be called back. By becoming aware of your actions and motivations, you can practice more conscious release of arrows, and bring better consequences (or karma).

"Your target is your life's purpose. Whenever you get ready to shoot an arrow, ask yourself out of your own deep wisdom, "Is what I'm going to do useful for my life's purpose? What will the consequences be? Does this option take me closer or farther from enlightenment?"

Though I'm not an archer like Beth, it occurs to me that the Swami's questions are well worth asking as I release speech and actions in my own life. Maybe you'll feel the same way.

kids catch fish! . . . .

Twelve miles from downtown Oklahoma City, Rusty Minick looked up, startled, from the geranium he was tending. His greenhouse had vibrated. It felt like an earthquake or a—an explosion. *Nah. Couldn't be.* But he turned on the office TV, and within minutes, saw people running through fire and smoke. Heard screams. Saw Oklahoma City's federal building in ruins. Newscasters' shocked voices said it was terrorist attack.

Like people everywhere, he couldn't believe it. Eyes glazed, Rusty watched the horror unfold. People buried in rubble. The day care center destroyed. And as he watched, he remembered another horror. A very personal one.

He was fourteen years old, a big, strapping kid with a dark brown crewcut. When he came home from school that day, the front door was locked. No, something blocked it. He pushed his way in. Blood everywhere. Fist to mouth. Gagging. No, Mom, no . . . a shot gun blast to her head. Murdered by his stepfather.

Days of shock. His dad arriving from California. Sobbing. And a few months later, his grandmother's sorrowful voice. "Rusty, it's your father, he's. . . " Hating to say it. Forced to. His father, depressed, had committed suicide.

"Come on, boy, we'll go fishing," said his Grandpa. He thought fishing was good for whatever ailed you, and it did help to sit in Grandpa's boat and throw out a line. Grandpa told stories and jokes. He made Rusty laugh. "Laughter is good medicine," Grandpa liked to say, "but fishing is the best medicine of all, and don't you forget it!"

And then, before Rusty's sixteenth birthday, Grandpa died. Rusty hadn't known he was sick. In two years, he'd lost the three people he loved most.

In 1969, the year his mother was murdered, no one thought about counseling or support groups for grieving kids. It was the same after his grandpa died. Rusty didn't know where to turn, and for a while, he crawled into a shell. But on weekends, he still went fishing.

He liked going up the creek or out on the lake in Grandpa's boat. It didn't matter much if he caught a fish. Sitting alone in the quiet, he remembered his grandpa's jokes and stories, and sometimes Grandpa seemed to be there with him, as if somehow they were still connected.

He wasn't sure exactly why or how, but fishing helped Rusty recover.

After high school, he went to work, saved his money, married Paula, a young widow with three children, and got on with life.

Through the years, though, he kept on fishing. It relaxed and comforted him. Out on the lake it was easy to talk to God, especially if something worried him. "Show me the way to go," he'd pray. Often Rusty felt as if he got an answer, sometimes from a good-news phone call or in a friend's encouraging letter.

Memories came flooding back as Rusty watched the tragic events unfold in Oklahoma City. Here were children losing their parents just as he'd lost his. Suddenly. Violently. He yearned to help.

About a week after the bombing, he fell asleep. He wakened in the middle of the night. Had a voice called his name? For an instant, he groped for the phone, but it hadn't rung. He fell asleep again. And again it seemed as if a voice woke him. "Rusty. You can help those kids. You've been down that road. You know what to do." The voice sounded so clear, so real, he almost woke his wife Paula to see if she heard it. Then he simply rolled over. But his face held a sleepy smile because suddenly he knew how to help.

Rusty remembered his peculiar dream when he woke the next morning. Right away he called Jimmy Houston, a television fishing pro on ESPN. Would Jimmy appear at a fishing derby for the kids who had lost someone in the bombing? "Sure," said Jimmy. Then Rusty began contacting other Oklahoma athletes. Between making calls and cutting through government red tape, his plan took months to achieve. But a year after the bombing, on a sunny May morning, forty-seven kids who had lost a relative or were themselves injured by the bomb blast, had come to Lake Arcadia to fish with sports stars.

The water was stocked with 200 hungry catfish, and as parents heard their children laugh, they smiled too. One dad said gratefully, "This is the most laughter I've heard since the bombing."

It was all the affirmation Rusty needed. A month later, on a donated charter bus, he took fifty kids to Lake Texoma to spend a day with pro fishing guides in their boats. Over the next four years, he arranged fifty-two outings for the children of the Oklahoma City bombing. His efforts won a "Point-of Light" award and letters from the President and U.S. Senators. And on 160 acres, Rusty's nonprofit foundation KIDS, WE CARE is building a permanent kids' fishing camp for children who have endured trauma.

It's a simple thing, really. Giving a kid a chance to fish. But Rusty, who's now a grandpa himself, believes it's true what his own grandpa told him so many years ago: "Laughter is good medicine, but fishing is the best medicine of all!"

COACH'S REFLECTION: In life's difficult times, often it's a simple gesture that brings balm to the soul. Rusty was helped in working through his own grief by the tranquility of water, the calm of fishing, and the restorative power of happy memories. When the opportunity came, he passed on to others the gift he had received. Writer Henri Nouwen coined the phrase, "the wounded healer." Those who have been wounded by similar experiences are most capable of offering support and understanding. Isn't this how the Holy Spirit acts in the world?

What simple activity has helped restore you in troubled times? Has a friend—or perhaps someone you didn't expect—become a source of comfort? How can you pass on a similar gift to someone else? Your answers can help you be part of the Holy Spirit at work in the world.

lake swimming, nature's comfort . . .

Upstate New York is a land of old mountains, heavy-leafed trees, and natural lakes. On the shore of one of those lakes in late June, freelance writer Erica Manfred hesitated. She saw no one. Green Lake basked silently in the summer sun while trees made patterns of dappled shade. The water, as it gently lapped the shore, seemed to whisper, *Come in, come in.*

She took off her sandals and climbed gingerly down the rocks that led to the water. Holding her breath, she happily plunged into the cold water. Swimming in a lake was like slipping into a happy childhood memory.

Slowly, she began to swim the crawl, arms lifting, falling, lifting again. The water flowed around her, soft, soothing, sensuous. Her strokes became surer. Breathe, kick, stroke four times, breathe, kick, stroke four times. . . . For the first time in months, she felt buoyant. *Free.* Free of the pain of betrayal. Free of her weight.

When her hand touched a raft on the lake's far side, she pulled herself up and sprawled, elated to have made it, relishing the tingle of water drops drying on her skin. She was tired, but pleasantly so. In the aftermath of personal rejection, swimming in a natural setting had comforted her as well as reminded her of her own strength. Suddenly, deliriously, almost as if the words were spoken aloud, she thought, "As long as there's a Green Lake, life is worth living."

Erica began swimming on every hot summer day she could get to the lake. The water cradled her with a womb-like feeling, especially when she reached the middle of the lake. Out in the middle, she felt safe. No one could reach her there.

Sometimes she rolled over, floating on her back awhile, luxuriating in the sensation of being untouchable. Clouds drifted past. She closed her eyes, letting emotions drift in and through her like the clouds . . . regret, anger, shame, disappointment . . . all the feelings bound up in her husband's announcing that he loved another woman.

Even her white-hot rage was somehow dissipated by the time she got out of the water. It was as if the

Lake spoke to her, consoling her, helping her to understand her life.

The Lake also reminded her she couldn't just quit. To reach the shore, eventually she had to roll over and get going again: *breathe, kick, stroke.*

She didn't set goals or try to swim fast. It was enough just to swim. To notice a dragon fly's darting motion. The flash as a fish jumped. To hear a woodpecker's cheerful rat-a-tat-tat. It was a deeply meditative experience

"I felt so discarded by my husband. My self-esteem had plummeted," she said. "But the more I swam, the more in touch I got with my body. And the more I began to understand myself. For years, I'd pretended my marriage some something it was not. I just kept eating and eating, pretending."

Now, beneath the comforting caress of sun and water, Erica saw her life more clearly. And slowly she began to heal.

COACH'S REFLECTION: I think the twenty-third psalm is so beloved because it offers us comfort. *"Yea, though I walk through the valley of the shadow, I will fear no evil . . . your rod and your staff, they comfort me."*

If you've suffered a painful rejection or loss, maybe now is a good time to ask, as Erica did, "What activity or what environment will bring me the most comfort?" A friend of mine calls skiing ". . . more than recreation. It's re-creation for me, especially when I'm hurting." A lot of people choose the simple act of walking. It's up to you.

But like the comfort foods of meat loaf and mashed potatoes, comfort exercise, too, has its place. What exercise makes you most comfortable?

one hundred percent soccer . . . . . .

My grandson Danny *loves* to play soccer. And his coach in Springfield, Missouri is equally passionate about the game. But the lessons Carl Rose teaches his players come from far more than soccer itself.

Carl was born in London fifty years ago, and, like most British kids, started kicking a soccer ball when he was only seven. But soccer is more than just kicking. It employs your whole body. It's how you use your eyes and your feet in a crisscrossing pattern, dribbling the ball, passing it off to a teammate, making the ball stop where and when you want it to. It's all about control. Teamwork. And how you position yourself.

Carl was a natural.

He liked getting to a field early, when dew was still on the grass and the air felt chilly. It never took long to warm up. He loved having someone dribble the ball to him, then exchanging passes and moving the ball along the field of play. He thrilled to the roller coaster excitement of a close game. "Like chugging up a hill—then *watch out*! Coming down fast."

He prized the exhilaration of getting near the goal, hearing the grunts of teammates, maybe some razzing from the other team. "Feeling so in tune with your mate that you didn't need to look, you knew he'd be there to get the ball when you put it out." Playing soccer was in

Carl's blood. At thirteen, he was invited to join a training club for future professional soccer players.

When his parents moved the family to Toronto, Carl was angry at first. "I felt as if my parents had ruined my dream to play professional soccer."

But Canadians like soccer too, and once again, Carl attracted attention. He won a spot playing offensive forward on the Canadian national team, and in 1976, experienced an athlete's dream—his team was chosen for the Montreal Olympics. He'll never forget the opening parade of nations, the torch bearer lighting the Olympic flame, the realization that 80,000 people were in the stands watching, while millions more watched on TV.

"I was so nervous before our first game, I think I went to the bathroom ten times in ten minutes," laughs Carl. Even though his team met defeat, nothing will ever take away the memory of *being* there. "I felt as if God had given me a gift, and I had used it well." He said a prayerful thank you.

The Olympics gave Carl his chance at another dream. He turned pro and played for a St. Louis team. Soccer isn't as popular in the U.S. as it is in the rest of the world, so while Carl earned a comfortable living, he never saw the big salaries of some pro athletes. But he was doing what he loved. He married, became a father, bought a house, and life seemed good.

Shortly before his team contract came up for renewal, Carl said to his wife Terri, "I think I'll check the gutter on the roof. It may be broken." As he clambered up their roof, his foot slipped. He lost his balance. His arms frantically pinwheeled, but it was too late. He saw the edge of the roof coming, felt himself go over, and—next thing he knew, he woke up in a hospital. He was partially paralyzed on his left side, blind in his left eye, and deaf in his left ear. For someone who played a professional sport, it was devastating news. *It's not fair,* he thought. *I have a child. I'm the family's breadwinner. How will we manage?*

The next ten months were an excruciating time of rehabilitation. For a long while, Carl felt consumed with anger at the turn life had taken. "Thank God Teri loved me enough to hang in there," he says. Together, they prayed for his healing, and gradually his paralysis did lessen. But his doctor said bluntly, "Carl, stop hoping you'll see again. You're blind in one eye. Accept it. Move on."

One day, as his son reached up to hug his daddy, Carl realized, *I still have so much. I need to be grateful for all I have.* Now he thinks his prayers for healing were answered by a healing of his spirit.

Playing professional soccer was out of the question, but maybe, thought Carl, he could give back something to the game he loved so much. In nearby Springfield, he opened a soccer club for young players: The Carl Rose Soccer Association.

That's where my grandson Danny met Carl. Carl has taught Danny a lot. Better ways to control the ball. Good defense and offense skills. But the most important lessons he teaches are the lessons for living that he's learned on the soccer field—and off of it.

COACH'S REFLECTION: Here's what Carl told me he teaches his players:

- Give one hundred percent in every game you play. If you lose, learn from your mistakes and move on. No one wins all the time.

- When you walk out of the locker room after a game, let the game go. It's done. Put it behind you.

- Take responsibility for yourself. Don't make excuses or blame others.

- Have faith in the goodness of God and count your blessings.

After talking to Carl, I wondered, "Am I a *one-hundred percenter*? Whatever the challenge, do I give my best?" Most of the time, if it's something important, I think I do. But sometimes my best adds up to less than 100 percent. Maybe in the past I did better because I was more rested. Maybe in the future I'll do better because I'll have more experience.

I've decided the real question is, "Am I giving my best *today*?" That's all that is required of any of us.

paddle prayer . . . .

I was a tourist, strolling along the shore of Lake Michigan, when I spied two dots of yellow bobbing on the water. I stopped to watch. The dots grew larger. Two women, their bright yellow kayaks enclosing them like fins, paddled toward shore. They reminded me of mermaids rising out of the waves. Water drops sparkled from the single paddle that each woman held aloft, then dipped.

I gazed across the broad expanse of water—which appeared to stretch as far as any ocean—and marveled at their temerity. As they pulled their kayaks ashore, I asked,

"How long were you out?"

One of the women glanced at her sports watch. She wore shorts and a tank top and her legs and arms looked strong. "About two hours."

Her friend nodded. Their small boats scrunched into the sand like two bananas.

The first woman, who introduced herself as Louise, told me they liked wilderness camping, and kayaks allowed them to reach places inaccessible by land. "This morning, though, we're just out for exercise."

In the distance, a dog barked. A small plane droned overhead. The Michigan breeze blew along my arms. We talked for a few more minutes. Curious, I asked, "What made you start kayaking?"

Louise took a drink from her canteen, gazed across the water, then looked at me.

"I was an over-achieving workaholic, climbing the ladder of success," she said. "And if that meant sixty-hour work-weeks and no outside life, well, I figured that's what it took. And then I got cancer."

After a year of radiation and chemotherapy, Louise had "a whole different perspective on life." She stopped her sixty-hour weeks. She started spending time outdoors. At first, just walking. Then, hikes with friends. Camping. Eventually, kayaking.

I asked her if kayaking, in the wake of cancer, held any kind of spiritual dimension.

She nodded. "I'm not a church-goer—but my illness made me realize I'm not running the show. There is a profound Mystery larger than I and somehow, it was part of the healing process. In my kayak, I sit low and close to the water, and when I lift my paddle, it's as if I'm part of the boat, the water, the sky, the whole mystery of creation." She raised her arms, brought them down, raised them again. "It seems natural to give thanks as I paddle. I'm so grateful for life."

"Paddle prayer," I said.

She smiled. "That's a good name for it."

COACH'S REFLECTION: On a day-to-day basis, does your life, like mine, often get sucked into the jam-packed "tyranny of the urgent"? Today's workplace, especially, is more demanding. And if you have to stay at work longer to get it all done, which may short-change family time, well, you might think, "So be it." Sometimes it takes a crisis—in Louise's case, her cancer—to remind us what really counts.

The next time someone says to you, "Don't work too hard," why not reply, "I won't." And then, *don't*. Keep your life in balance. One of the best ways to do it is to visit God's natural world as a regular part of your agenda. When you breathe nature's clean wind and smell a fresh pine forest or when you walk along a beach at sunrise, your soul responds. It's easier then to sort out what's important from what isn't. And you won't need a kayak paddle in your hand to say a prayer of gratitude for all you have.

swimming in rough waters . . . .

Marcie McGahey Cecil is an effervescent woman, with blonde curls, blue eyes, and a laugh that bubbles

MEDITATION IN MOTION

up like really good champagne, all gathered around an incisive, creative mind. On any morning, you're likely to see her leave her small California beach apartment in a short-sleeved wet suit, trot down outside stairs past the bright painted mural on one side of her building, and head for La Jolla's famous Cove, a small, exquisite beach tucked between sandstone cliffs.

At the beach, she hails her swim partner, pulls on fins and goggles, and wades quickly into the bone-chilling water. Bright yellow and white buoys mark distance and direction. Marcie and her partner plan to do a rough-water swim—a half mile out, then back again.

Life has a way of circling back on itself. As a bouncy teenager, Marcie was a junior Olympics swimmer. Then, her biggest fan was her mother, as vibrant a woman as Marcie is today. Marcie's mom, Mary, felt a deep Catholic devotion to the Blessed Mother and encouraged the same devotion in her daughter.

After Marcie grew up, life's meandering trail led her away from the ocean to the Midwest. Her childhood Catholicism was put on hold. She became the imaginative genius behind a successful company that created large corporate events for clients around the world. She married, watched her two boys grow up, went through the pain of divorce, and then watched her beautiful mother die of systemic lupus.

In her forties, Marcie learned that she, too, had lupus. Like all auto-immune diseases, lupus has a bewildering array of symptoms, and it affected Marcie's eyes. Only a corneal transplant saved her from total blindness in one eye.

finding healing

Serious illness can make you re-examine your life. Marcie felt as if she were being pulled to the ocean, back to the water she had loved as a child. She sold her business for a comfortable sum and moved to southern California. Friends told her she was brave to make such a drastic move, but to Marcie, it wasn't brave. She *had* to do it. Had to spend time alone. Had to think about her future and what life now held for her.

A few blocks from her beach apartment she noticed a small Catholic church: *Mary Star of the Sea*. As if drawn by an unseen hand, Marcie walked inside one day. Blue and red votive candles flickered. She smelled incense. Saw an icon of Mary as the Blessed Mother. Instinctively, Marcie made the sign of the cross and knelt down. She remembered her mother's soft voice as she prayed her Rosary. In a whisper, Marcie began, "Hail Mary, full of grace . . . " As she prayed the familiar words, she felt as if she had come home again.

Over the next year, Marcie continued working with her doctors. She took the prescribed corticosteroids, but she also studied nutrition and changed her diet. She exercised and incorporated prayerful meditation into her daily life. Her body grew stronger. And one day, doctors gave her good news. Her lupus symptoms had subsided!

In a joyful mood, Marcie drove past La Jolla's Cove. She noticed two swimmers in wet suits plunging into the ocean. They weren't scuba divers. They were swimmers. Instantly, Marcie knew she wanted to swim there, too.

Rough water swimming is just that—you cut through swells and waves. It's cold and hard going. Depending on shifts in the current, undertows can make it hazardous.

But from the beginning, Marcie loved it.

Swimming in the ocean gave her time to think. There was very little sound, other than her own arms, lifting and falling as she stroked through the water. About a quarter mile off shore, she would carefully swim through a yellow kelp forest waving gently in the water. It grew up from a deep underwater canyon floor, and the tube-like strands with their foot-long leaves could be dangerous if you got twisted in them. But she loved the way the strands felt against her skin. So soft, like silk.

Through her goggles, Marcie would see the Garibaldi, looking like giant goldfish; schools of tiny senorita fish; and sometimes a flat halibut or zebra perch. She never felt afraid.

One day, when her swim partner didn't show up, Marcie decided to make a quick swim on her own. She'd be done in forty minutes. No big deal.

She was concentrating on her strokes and watching the ocean life through her goggles when she heard a man yelling. She lifted her head. A scuba diver pointed. "Watch—" And then it was on her, a huge nine-foot swell that drove her under water with such force it was like being caught in a giant washing machine. The powerful wave knocked off her goggles and pulled her down at least ten feet. She managed to swim to the surface, suck in air, and then another wave hit her, with more waves right behind it. As she was pulled down again, Marcie cried out. Not aloud, but in a small, inner voice. "Blessed Mother, I need help!"

Once more, she struggled to reach the surface. As another wave engulfed her, she heard a lifeguard's shout. "Grab the buoy!" He threw her a buoy as he dove from his lifeguard boat. Then he pulled her through the waves into shallow water.

The experience convinced her not to swim again without a partner, but it didn't scare her off. With a luminous look, Marcie says softly, "Swimming in rough water is a special achievement. In childhood, I swam long hours, practicing to compete, but I swam in pools, with chlorine in my nostrils. It was a very controlled, man-made environment.

Illness has helped me see—and accept—how little control I actually have in life. I know it's possible that my lupus symptoms may return. The ocean is uncontrolled, too. Maybe I like swimming there because it's God's environment and I'm willing now to turn my life over to God."

She smiles. Mischievously. "But I'm always willing to ask the Blessed Mother to intercede."

COACH'S REFLECTION: I know that living a God-centered life means surrendering your will to God's. Yet life's paradox is surely revealed in Marcie's story. She struggled against the waves that threatened to drown her—and simultaneously, chose to swim in waters that couldn't be controlled.

St. Benedict, whose wise Monastic Rule has influenced western thought since the eighth century, wrote that seeking God is about making progress toward living in total dependence on God's grace, but that Grace doesn't substitute for our activity. It simply puts God at the heart of what we do.

Perhaps that's why sports of all kinds convey such powerful meaning. You prepare, practice, and play with all you've got. At the same time you know that once the ball is hit, the stroke has been taken, the swim has begun, anything is possible. Ultimately, players can only surrender to the outcome.

Here's a simple reminder of what it means to surrender. Clench one fist, then gently turn it, and open it. When you open your hands it symbolizes your readiness to receive whatever life brings you.

whispering to horses . . . .

The horse stood fourteen hands high and pawed the ground nervously. It shied from Maggie and rolled its eyes. "Poor thing was treated very cruelly," said Terry, who had told Maggie about the rescued animal.

Maggie held out her hand. "Careful," warned Terry, "He likes to bite."

But Maggie wasn't afraid. She regarded the horse with a practiced eyes. Half Arabian, half saddlebred. A beautiful chestnut color. "What's his name?"

"Dreamcatcher."

"*Dreamcatcher*?" Maggie smiled. All her life she'd believed in pursuing—and catching—her dreams. But her doctor's recent diagnosis threatened to sideswipe Maggie's dreams. She looked at the horse more carefully. "How about it, Dreamcatcher? Think we might help one another?"

Maggie Finerock's specialty was mediating disputes between people and companies and offering diversity training. She loved her work, even if it meant international travel and, occasionally, eighty-hour work weeks. But recently, her doctors had told her she had chronic fatigue syndrome, possibly picked up during a Peace Corps stint in Nepal, and CFS was depleting her once prodigious energy. Sometimes she was so weary, it was all she could do to finish delivering a seminar.

Besides her work, Maggie loved horses. She had started working with them when she was twelve, and helping out at a summer camp near her Ohio hometown. When she stroked a velvety nose or wrapped her arms around a horse's neck, her heart stirred. She felt connected in a way she felt with no other animal.

Even as a kid, she had intuitively felt something was wrong with the traditional idea of breaking a horse's spirit in order to control the animal. Years later, as an adult, she made time in her busy schedule to train in the natural horsemanship methods developed by Pat Parelli, a well-known Colorado "horse whisperer."

Natural horsemanship has a Zen-like quality. It works on the premise that horses are happy to do what a human wants, so if a horse isn't responding, seek first to understand *why* rather than get confrontational. Some problems occur because a rider gives cues that are foreign to the horse. Or an apparent behavior issue may really be a discomfort problem. The horse has been fitted with a poorly fitting saddle or its gums are sore from the bridle.

Most of all, you must know yourself. If you're clear about what you want, you can develop a deep harmony between you and your horse. *"Know thyself first."*

Using natural horsemanship methods, Maggie began to create a bond with Dreamcatcher. She gentled him, talked to him, assured him he never had to fear another cruel owner. She rode him through Missouri's hill country, listening to the summer hum of cicadas, smelling the pungent horseflesh, spying rabbits and, occasionally, in the distance, a deer. As she rode, Maggie's own emotions quieted. The frustrations of her disease began to dissipate. When she rode Dreamcatcher, she felt as if he understood her body, and despite the fatigue that is so debilitating from CFS, she felt stronger after her rides.

In the same way Dreamcatcher was learning to trust her, Maggie was learning to tolerate and trust the changes in her body. Gradually, she realized that slowing down and living more quietly didn't mean she was giving up on life. Perhaps now, she thought, it was time to mentor others instead of doing it all herself.

"Owning Dreamcatcher reminded me that even when a dream turns out differently than you imagined, it can still be worthwhile," said Maggie. "And it's still up to each of us to catch our own dreams."

COACH'S REFLECTION: *Know thyself.* It's such a brief phrase to express something that takes a lifetime to fully accomplish! But I've learned self-knowledge is a necessary part of any spiritual journey.

finding healing

Physical exercise helps in the quest for self-knowledge because it doesn't let us fool ourselves. You can't pretend to ski a steep run or jump a high hurdle or sail a boat. And your horse will know if you're not authentic. Outdoor activity, says Robert Schultheis "... pares us down to the blazing bare bones, to the beautiful terrible core of it all."

It takes courage to seek your core. It may change your life, especially if it causes you to recognize a dream that you had earlier pushed aside. A dream you thought would never come true. Seeking a dream can change a life. It's also what gives life a richer meaning. As Maggie said, it's up to each of us to catch our own dreams.

The first step surely must be *knowing thyself.*

red blood, black belt . . . .

She never expected the attack. Sandy Warshaw was headed for the swimming pool at her athletic club, a mile from her New York apartment, when something heavy struck her from behind. She reeled from the impact. A hand—the fingernails short and grubby— yanked at her purse-strap, and a guttural voice snarled, "Give it to me, lady!" When Sandy tried to jump away, she was struck again. This time she fell. Something sticky and warm trickled into her eye. She blinked and yelled, but the man—a blur of old sneakers, denims, nondescript shirt—had cut her purse strap and was running toward Central Park. She never saw him again.

The gash in her head required ten stitches. For the first time in her adult life, Sandy felt frightened about living in the city. When a friend urged her to learn self-defense, Sandy agreed. She signed up first for a course in self-defense. Later, she joined a karate class.

By happenstance, Sandy joined a Japanese karate-do school, World Seido Karate. Founded by Tadashi Nakamura, the focus is not on competition or even on self-defense, but on deepened integration of body and spirit. Students are taught how to control their minds and emotions as well as their bodies; how to know themselves and show respect for themselves as well as for others.

Her instructor explained that martial arts mimic the power of nature, where dynamic action (karate's physical moves) is balanced with perfect silence. "It is like a hurricane in which violent winds surround a perfectly still inner eye." Each class started and ended with the inner quiet of meditation.

After attending three classes a week for several years, Sandy, who had started as a white belt advanced through a brown belt. Eventually, a black belt. Each promotion also required a written essay about what she was learning in life.

As an obedient daughter in a 1950s Jewish household in Scarsdale, she had followed her family's expectations to marry and have children. At forty-two, a mastectomy reminded her that life is not forever. A few years later, her marriage floundered. Her grown children were living their own lives. Sandy began to realize that something had always been missing in her life, or perhaps unacknowledged. She could almost, but not quite, glimpse it out of the corner of her eye.

After a struggle, she finally admitted the truth. She was not the proper heterosexual Jewish girl her parents had raised. In the essay for her black belt, she wrote, "I've learned to give up the protection of my childhood defenses. I'm willing, at last, to live as my true self." She began to tentatively explore a loving relationship with another woman, and joined a synagogue that ministered to New York's gay and lesbian community.

Sandy now lives with her partner. She's also a doting grandmother, and is actively engaged in the twin fights against ageism and homophobia. "I'm actually grateful for the mugging," she told me, "because without it, I might never have discovered martial arts and karate-do. That discipline helped me acknowledge the reality of who I am."

COACH'S REFLECTION: In childhood I was taught the great commandment: "Love God and love one another as you love yourself." But for many years I can't honestly say I loved myself. I didn't even *know* myself. And how can you love someone you don't really know? I judged myself against the expectations placed on me by parents and society, just as Sandy did.

But Shakespeare said it well: *"To thine own self be true."*

A major part of anyone's spiritual journey is learning to know yourself so you can be true to the authentic person you are. Some people never take the risk because it may mean standing up against the dictates of family or friends. But it's the only way to truly live.

Physical disciplines that combine a meditative element, such as yoga, tai chi, or karate-do, often help us take the risk. As you exercise, ask yourself the question: "Who am I? Who is the person I sometimes glimpse out of the corner of my eye?"

Don't push for an answer. Allow it to unfold.

4
EXPANDING YOUR
BOUNDARIES

courage to be clumsy . . . .

The summer I was fifteen, I took tennis lessons. Well, that's not quite accurate. I took *one* tennis lesson. I can still see myself, tall, big-boned, gawky, not very well-coordinated, and prone to bump into things. ("Barbara, don't be so clumsy!" my mother would exclaim.). It was a warm June morning and I was hunched over a tennis racket on a court near our family's home in Virginia.

Six of us, all beginners, all girls, were trying to learn the rudiments of whacking a ball across a net. Denise, a year older than I and one of the *really* popular girls in school, hit her ball with a rich *thwack* and watched it sail across the court. She smiled happily. Now it was my turn. I swung my racket, and *thwump*, the ball dribbled off court. "No, no!" yelled the instructor. "Bring your racket back this way—" and he hit the ball with the same resounding *thwack* as Denise. I nodded and tried again. Another dribble. One of the girls giggled, and I felt myself flush. Then she stepped up, nicely served her ball, and got an approving nod from the instructor. I wiped sweat off my forehead. When my turn came again, I clenched my fist around my racket and carefully brought it back. All eyes were watching. I swung. Tripped. Tried to catch myself. And *thwump*. The ball dribbled off court. I wanted to disappear. *You big oaf. You'll never learn to play.* I felt awkward and incredibly *clumsy*.

At the end of our lesson, the instructor gave each of us a summary of our progress. He looked at me with what I perceived as a doubtful expression. "This is not a natural sport for you. You'll have to work hard, Barbara. But I *think* you can learn." To me, his words implied just the opposite: *"Yeah, sure, I'll be surprised if you <u>ever</u> get that ball across the net."*

And that ended tennis for me. I never went back. For years, I refused to try any sport that involved eye-hand coordination. I couldn't stand the thought of people watching me fall on my face.

Last year, while on cross-country road trip, I stopped in Boulder, Colorado, to visit my long-time friend, Laura. When we met as young women, Laura was lithe, limber, beautiful. Long before I discovered the joys of exercise, she skied, hiked, and played avid tennis.

Two years ago, Laura was diagnosed with a rare rheumatoid condition that has forced her to end many of her cherished physical activities. "I'm worse," she said, nearly spilling her cup of coffee. Her smile was rueful. "Clumsy as all get out. I have more trouble holding onto things than Peter Sellers ever did. Quite a comedown for someone who always thought of herself as graceful."

I poured cream into my coffee. Laura's hand, I noticed, shook as she lifted her cup. But her voice was strong. "I decided to just deal with it—without shame or frustration. So now when I knock over a chair or objects drop from my hands, I'm not surprised. In fact, I actually *expect* that everything I touch will go awry."

Inexplicably, as she spoke, a long-forgotten memory flashed: of me and my one-and-only tennis lesson. I seemed to feel, again, the sweat on my brow. The sun on my neck. The instructor's voice. The *thwacking* sound of his ball, and the *thwump* of my poor dribble. More than anything else on that long-ago

June morning, I had hated feeling *clumsy*. So to avoid discomfort, I never went back.

But Laura can't do that. She's stuck. *"I simply deal with it—without shame or frustration."*

It occurred to me that at fifteen, I lacked Laura's courage to be clumsy. Like a typical teen, I was way too self-conscious. And for years afterward, I shied away from anything that seemed to demand coordination. But as I reached for Laura's hand, I wondered, for one brief, wistful moment: What might have happened to my tennis game if I had gone back for lesson number two?

Then a happy thought occurred. Who says it's too late? I could sign up for tennis lessons *now*.

COACH'S REFLECTION: Author Jerry Lynch, Ph.D., in his book on the Zen of sports, points out that when you relax and are patient, a situation may gradually unfold in your favor. Whatever the activity, perhaps the right prayer is this one: "O Lord, give me the courage to be clumsy, and the faith to keep on trying."

cycling lessons . . . .

"I started bicycling to escape stress," says Nancy Thrutchley, picking up her latte. She has a Julia Roberts kind of smile and a body that's trim and lithe. "What I learned are rules for living." Thinking about my own bicycling, I wait, curious to hear more.

Three years after a difficult divorce, Nancy was laid off from her job. She was desperate for some kind of activity to relieve the pressure, if only for a little while.

With "crummy knees," running, skiing, hiking, even tennis were out of reach, so she walked into a bicycle shop one August morning, pointed to a used hybrid bike, and said, "I'll take it."

Sipping her latte, Nancy laughs. "I was such a novice! I didn't know enough to buy a helmet or gloves or a bicycle pump. But I made a date with myself to bicycle on Saturday to a quaint little town a few miles from where I lived. I'd have lunch and bicycle back. Piece of cake, I thought."

Except that what seemed a "few miles" by car were actually twenty, which made the round trip forty miles, and Nancy had never cycled more than five miles in her life. Going out didn't seem too bad, "because I had a tailwind helping me. But what do tailwinds turn into once you turn around? Headwinds!"

The ride home was tough. Nancy kept telling herself, "I can make it. And If I have to get off and walk, that's okay. I can walk eighteen miles . . . sixteen miles . . . fourteen miles. . . ." Finally, she pedaled into her driveway with hands so numb from gripping her handlebars she couldn't work her front door key. But she had learned a vital life lesson: you can go a lot farther than you think you can.

We're seated in a local coffee house. A cell phone rings at a table near us. Nancy glances over, returns her gaze to me. "I've learned a lot more from bicycling about how to live than I ever learned from the fire and brimstone church I grew up in."

Nancy bought a helmet and gloves, heard about a local bicycling group, and went on a Saturday ride with them. "Of course, they were hunched over road bikes while I was perched on my hybrid like the Wicked Witch in the Oz movie. Didn't take long to realize I needed a different kind of bike." She bought a used road bike, and continued to ride with the group. Their friendship provided just the right support as her legal battles continued. She also came to realize another life lesson: "When you're a parent going through a difficult time, you'll take better care of your kids if you also take care of yourself."

Picking up a paper napkin, Nancy jots some notes. "I think God brings into our lives what we need as we need it. Not before. I've come to trust in that. I think it's why I started cycling when I did." Abruptly, she looks at her watch and jumps up.

"Uh-oh, Barb. Gotta go." She hands me her napkin. "But here are some more lessons I've learned." I watch her through the coffee house window. Instead of getting in a car, she climbs on her bicycle and pedals off. I smile. Somehow I'm not surprised.

COACH'S REFLECTION: I can't say it any better than Nancy.

Here are her *Rules for Bicycling and for Life*:

① When you're bicycling into a headwind, accept it. Embrace it. It makes you stronger. "I've accepted that somethings will not change, and I just have to deal with them. But dealing with adversity has made me stronger in other situations. God really doesn't give you more than you can handle."

② You can do what seems impossible. "Making it back on that first forty-mile ride convinced me of that!"

③ When you're headed up a steep hill, don't look all the way up or you'll get discouraged. "I pay attention to the white line on my left. The top of the hill will come in its own good time."

④ Prepare. Shift gears *before* the hill. Drink *before* you're thirsty and eat before you're hungry. "Otherwise you could bonk." *Bonking* is a bicycling term. It occurs when a rider feels suddenly light-headed and sick, and comes from dehydration when you forget to drink your water. Bicyclists drink *before* they're thirsty so their bodies are continually replenished. If you think about it, prayer works the same way.

⑤ Don't worry about how far you've come or how far you have to go. Notice the beauty of where you are. For a while, Nancy obsessed over mileage—was she going faster per mile? More miles per hour? Then her mileage computer broke, and instead of fixing it, she decided, "I'll just enjoy each moment I'm riding."

gymnast! . . . .

In 1956, when the Olympics opened in Melbourne, Australia, sports headlines vied with grimmer news. Three weeks earlier, Soviet tanks had rolled into Budapest and crushed a national Hungarian uprising against communist rule. Nearly 200,000 Hungarians fled into exile.

Marta Nagy, a sixteen-year-old member of Hungary's Olympic gymnastic team, made her own momentous decision. When the Olympics ended, she and other Hungarian athletes defected in Australia and then went to America.

Eager to help the talented young athletes, several American universities offered them scholarships so they could stay in the U.S. That's how, in the spring of 1957, Marta reached the University of Colorado in Boulder where I met her.

My college sorority, Kappa Kappa Gamma, had invited Marta to live in the Kappa house as a guest. Vicki, a Kappa who roomed with Marta and who became her good friend, remembers their first meeting. "She had a cardboard suitcase filled with a few clothes, a funny haircut, no money, and she spoke no English." She missed her family (whom she wouldn't see again for eight years), and despite her father's admonition, "Go, Marta! Make a better life for yourself," she worried that her defection might cause government reprisals against family members.

Even so, this tiny young woman—she was just five feet tall—had such a brisk, decisive manner, it was clear she understood: *it's up to me to take care of myself and I can do it.* "She didn't have enough money to buy herself a lipstick," remembers Vicki, "but with the help of some people from *Sports Illustrated* magazine, she got a summer job filing in a California office. She was able to earn some money and when she came back to school in the fall, she enrolled in a full course load, determined to earn her degree."

Marta's athletic discipline is what sustained her. She worked out regularly in the university gymnasium, stretching, tumbling, swinging, releasing, turning, jumping, leaping. Practicing routines on the asymmetrical bars, the balance beam and the horse vault helped her keep her emotional balance.

Once, after sitting in a lecture hall feeling *so stupid!* because she didn't understand enough English to grasp the subtleties of what the lecturer was saying, Marta went to the gym and executed a series of perfect back handsprings, lifting her arms in triumph as she finished. She wondered if she would ever have a chance to compete again at Olympic level. (It was not to be. Although Senator Barry Goldwater tried to get U.S. citizenship for Marta in time for her to join the U.S. team in the 1960 Olympics, he didn't succeed.)

Marta experienced a lot of support from the Kappas. Every Christmas, she went with Vicki to Vicki's family home in Florida. She laughed along with others at her malapropisms as she struggled with English "She had a hard time with the '*th-*' sound," says Vicki, "so every night before bedtime, I made her practice saying '*theopholis thistle.*' Usually we wound up laughing hysterically."

In 1960, after she succeeded in earning her degree, she and Vicki backpacked through Europe. They went to the Olympics in Rome, a bittersweet experience for Marta. Then, since she was still politically unable to return to her homeland, Marta stayed in Vienna while Vicki traveled into Hungary to bring back news from Marta's family. Her beloved father died before she saw her family again, and she still feels heartache about that. Yet Marta is at peace with her decision to reach out to freedom.

For Marta, building her new life was like becoming a champion athlete. She might have the support of teammates and coach, but it was still up to her to do the tough personal training. Like many athletes, she went deep within herself to find her inner strength. Yet Marta realizes now that her body and spirit were always closely connected. What she once considered her athletic discipline was also her spiritual discipline.

I was happy to learn that Marta's life turned out so well. Through Vicki, she met the man she later married, and after their children grew up, the Wacheters retired to Boulder, so Marta has come full circle, back to where she started in America. "This is my home now," Marta told me. "I'm as American as apple pie." Then she laughed. "In spite of my accent."

COACH'S REFLECTION: Not everyone has the kind of major upheaval in life that Marta went through, but every life contains some unexpected event. A twist that wasn't planned.

Athletic discipline is an excellent sacred metaphor, says Chungliang Al Huang in *Working Without, Working Within.* He says it helps a person focus on becoming calm and quiet in the midst of turmoil. Many people have told me it helps them to run or walk or swim when they're upset. I've used my bicycle more than once to peddle my way to calm.

The value of any regular discipline—whether it's exercise, meditation, even gardening or cooking—is that it's already in place when lives erupt in sudden chaos. Like the fire drills practiced in schools, muscle memory takes over when emotions are wrought, so you can still perform. In Marta's case, her athletic discipline helped her eventually thrive.

It's good to ask: "In what situations do I show the most discipline? How disciplined am I in prayer and sports?"

the kingdom of handball . . . .

I see them in my athletic club every afternoon. The handball crowd, a group of men, some in their seventies, others closer to forty, but all with lean bodies and strong arms, because you run around the court a lot when you're hitting a two-inch hard rubber ball with nothing but a glove on your hand. Tom Bembynista is one of the forty-something players, a gregarious podiatrist who started playing about six years ago.

Handball originated where golf did—in Scotland—and aficionados say it's even more challenging. It's played on the same courts used by racquetball, but moves even faster. You put the ball in play by wrapping a gloved hand around it and *slinging* it at the court's far wall. Then watch out! Where will it bounce? How fast? Players—two or four to a court—run forward. Backward. Laterally. Always in pursuit of a ball that can hit speeds of seventy miles per hour. Dive for it! Sidearm a kill shot close to the floor. Overhand a defensive shot. And make sure you're wearing protective glasses.

Timing and technique are everything in handball, and the unique challenge is—you use both hands. Just try training your non-dominant hand to have the same power and coordination as your dominant hand.

It's tough. But unless you can do it, unless you can become at least semi-ambidextrous, you'll never be a handball player.

Tom learned his handball basics from a longtime enthusiast at the athletic club. Lou explained the strategies that could help him reach a winning twenty-one points. And he warned him it would be a steep learning curve. ". . . But once you get it, you won't let this sport go," he promised. And that's exactly what happened.

It took Tom, a guy with good eye-hand coordination, who had played serious baseball into his mid-thirties, about five years to become "fairly competent" in handball. Because it's so challenging, the numbers of players are small—about 40,000 total in the U.S.—and that gives handball the flavor of a unique fraternity. *We've got the right stuff.*

(There are female handball players, especially in the collegiate ranks, but most players in Tom's league are men.)

For Tom, it's become much more than a game. Handball players make up a community unlike any he has experienced with other sports. "Anywhere in the country, you can go and be welcomed," he says. And although players are competitive in the court, they are universally supportive of one another as they wait for courts, or travel together to tournaments, or even, as with Tom's group, donate funds to build their own outdoor court to use in the summer. "We care about each other," says Tom. Older players support younger ones. Young players honor their elders. "And when I talk to older guys—those in their seventies, one guy who's eighty—a light comes into their eyes.

Ask 'em about handball, and they talk faster and stand straighter. It's like watching them get young again."

COACH'S REFLECTION: Tom's own enthusiasm reminds me of what I know about the word "enthuse." It comes from the Greek *en theo*—and means *spirit within*. If Tom's an example, handball players are a spirited group. And perhaps, in their own way, spirit-led.

As he talked about handball's unique community, I thought about communities I've known that have warmly cared about their members. When I was a Navy fighter pilot's wife, I lived the slogan, "The Navy takes care of its own." After nine-eleven, the whole world saw how New York firefighters supported their own. And, surprisingly, I think about the community of early Christians—how small their number was in the beginning, how set apart they were, and how they cared for one another. All of us belong to some neighborhood or some community, and perhaps we should ask ourselves, "Am I supportive enough? Am I reaching out to those who need help in my community?"

inward bound. . . . .

Sandra Fisher couldn't help it. She cried out in pain. Her three companions looked back, concerned, as Sandra bent to massage her quadriceps. They were on their final Outward Bound exercise—an eighty-five-mile trek through the Cascade Mountains in upstate

Washington—all the way to the Canadian border and back.

Sandra, thirty-five, newly separated in her marriage and raising two young sons, had come on this wilderness adventure to test herself. "Challenge your perceived limits. Learn to know yourself," the brochure had said. Sandra hoped it might help her decide if she should try a new career after a decade of teaching high school. And maybe it would give her a new perspective for the difficult times ahead.

Outward Bound deliberately places participants in stressful situations, both physical and mental, challenging them to overcome obstacles. Teamwork and trust are essential.

Her team of four had been handed an old Indian map and told to find the trails they needed through the mountains. Eager to meet the challenge, they moved out fast. Too fast apparently, because now Sandra's leg muscles were locked into a tight spasm. Every time she moved, pain jabbed. *Darn, I'll hold the others back*, she thought.

Sandra was a natural leader—always had been—and she had willingly helped others as their Outward Bound group confronted each new wilderness test. She liked helping others; it was one of her strengths as a teacher.

But to need help herself? *No way.*

Dave and Jim, two of her teammates, had already back-tracked to help her. "I can manage," said Sandra. "I just have to go very slowly." She limped down the trail, stopping often to deal with pain. Finally she accepted their offer to massage her legs, feeling guilty for her own weakness. With every fiber of her being she wanted to say, "Don't wait for me. You go on." But this wasn't a walk in the park. Her companions couldn't leave her alone in the wilderness. They were a team and had to go on together.

Telling me about it later, she grimaced. "I hated being so helpless and dependent." She managed the steeper trails by walking backwards down hill. And gradually, thankfully, her muscle spasms did lesson.

Still, their progress was much slower than planned and they had to eliminate some trails altogether. "It was a very humbling experience," she said.

As a result, Sandra took away the opposite of what most people learn on Outward Bound. Her biggest challenge lay in *not* achieving, and in her forced acceptance of help from others. For someone who liked to lead, it was a difficult lesson.

After returning to New York, she did change careers. She earned a graduate degree in Exercise Physiology, and became director of Fitness and Health at the YWCA of New York City.

Many of the women she counseled came timidly. Some were overweight, some were clumsy, some had low self esteem, some had never tried to exercise and didn't know if they could do it. Every woman had different needs, different bodies, and was at a different place in her life.

"Before my experience on Outward Bound, I would have been out in front leading the women, but not necessarily understanding their vulnerabilities," said Sandra. "But now I had a more appreciation for how they felt. I was a better counselor." She showed an instinct for guiding each woman to the right exercise and the right trainer for her.

After serving as the YW director, she started her own wellness business designing motivational and educational programs. Now she travels internationally and gives motivational talks on managing stress, personal marketing and leadership to organizations. "My masters degree in physiology gave me skills," she said, "but it was that hike for Outward Bound that gave me empathy, as well as strength to go on, in spite of obstacles."

COACH'S REFLECTION: For years and years, I was a lot like Sandra. Ask me to lead or show the way, and I could do it. But I hated to ask for help and was fiercely independent. Or maybe I was just afraid. Afraid to be seen as occasionally weak. Afraid I wouldn't be accepted. Afraid that friends would scatter if I showed I was needy.

Bravery wears many garments. You might brave a fire to save someone's life, or speak out for justice when it isn't popular. Or as Sandra did, you might find it takes a lot of courage to gracefully accept the help you need from others.

I've often heard, "It's better to give than to receive." But perhaps what is really meant is this: "It's EASIER to give than to receive." In giving, we hold onto the power. Receiving makes us vulnerable. It takes special grace to receive in the right spirit.

Is it hard for you to ask for help? If so, think about what holds you back. What are you afraid will happen if you're on the receiving end? How can you address that fear?

orienteering: finding yourself . . . . .

In Washington, D.C., my daughter Sony and I were touring the Smithsonian, eager to see a particular art exhibit. A guard pointed down the main hallway. "Just walk to the other end of the building, ladies. You can't miss it."

Sure enough, at the other end, a sign announced what we were looking for. My daughter put a hand on my arm. "Mom," she said, and her voice was both amused and amazed, "I never realized before how important it is for you to *always* know exactly where you are. This was a straight shot, and still, you asked three people along the way if we were headed in the right direction!"

I laughed as heartily as she did. It was a behavior quirk *I* didn't know I had.

It is stressful not to know where you are, especially if, like me, you seem to be missing a natural sense of direction. That's why I listened in open-mouthed wonder to Betsy Betros, a Kansas City woman who *deliberately* gets lost and then tries to find her way home.

Betsy is a tail woman in her forties who loves the sport of orienteering. It's sometimes called the "thinking sport" because it involves map reading and decision-making along with a physical workout.

"It's a spiritual exercise, too," says Betsy. Her smile lights up her whole face. "Because it takes me out of my daily trappings and stops all my inner voices (the *musts*, the *shoulds*, the *can'ts*). The wheels in my head grow quiet. I become more aware of details—the flowers, insects, sun on my skin, the sky. It's as if my body becomes *saturated* with nature, so I feel totally in the moment."

I try to imagine getting lost on purpose.

"Not the sport for me," I say weakly.

"But it's not just about getting lost," says Betsy. "It's a willingness to be alone in nature and the confidence that you can wind up where you plan. You don't need experience and you can do it at any age as long as you can translate a two-dimensional map into a three-dimensional universe."

At orienteering meets, she explains, the object is to run, walk, ski or mountain bike to a series of points shown on a map, choosing routes that will get you to the course's end in record time. Points are marked with flags. You prove you've been there by punching your course-card.

"It isn't competitive the way some sports are," says Betsy, "because you're competing with yourself." The only expectations at an orienteering meet are those you place on yourself. Navigation is the key skill. You find where you are on a map, then create your own route to the next point. At every point you make a new decision about which way to go. "You take responsibility for yourself," says Betsy.

What happens if you *can't* figure a way out?

Someone will come look for you. At meets, everyone is required to sign in, so at the end of a meet, organizers can tell if someone goes missing.

With a slightly rueful chuckle, she admits it happened once to her. "I've always scoffed when someone says, 'I went around in circles' but in the middle of a meet in a large St. Louis park, I got disoriented. I couldn't read my map. Then I got panicky and didn't believe my compass. I started huffing and puffing across the terrain and when I came up over a hill—what a shock! I saw that I'd gone in circles and was back where I started. It scared me. And humbled me, too."

But she also learned that when you feel lost, if you take a deep breath, center yourself, and get out of panic mode, you often discover the right way to go.

COACH'S REFLECTION: Betsy said that orienteers create their own routes. We do the same in our lives. At each turning point, we make new decisions about which way to go. I think one of the big challenges is to recognize when you are at a crossroads.

Remember Tom Hanks in the movie *Castaway*? His character's decision to leave his fiancé at Christmas because his employer called changed his life forever. His plane went down and he was cast away on a deserted island for four years. His fiancé married another man and had a baby. At the end of the movie Hanks is standing at another crossroads. This time at least he *knows* he's at a crossroads. Often we don't.

The good thing about being centered in God means that even when you don't know if you've made the right decision, you can hold the same trust that Trappist monk Thomas Merton expressed when he wrote, ". . . *ultimately God will lead me by the right road though I may know nothing about it.*"

If you're not ready to sign up for an orienteering meet, let me suggest another way to build faith muscles. Next weekend, go on an old-fashioned Sunday drive along a two-lane highway you've never traveled before. Leave map and goals behind. Notice how comfortable you are with the experience. And notice what unexpected gifts you encounter along the way.

skydiving: soul-thriving . . . .

Skydiving, for Kate Griesser, is a sport intimately connected with her sense of God. "Being able to float through earth's atmosphere is like a treat from the Creator," she says. "When you skydive, you team up with Nature. It demands your attention, so you're focused totally in the moment, and being so focused brings a feeling of peace—with yourself and with the earth.

"Even the danger is a healthy reminder that I'm mortal. You consciously choose life when you pull your ripcord." Her eyes hold a faraway light. "Do you know that when you jump in central Florida on a clear day, you can see *both* coasts? It's an awesome feeling."

Kate, petite and pretty, but with strong hands, saw her first skydiving demo in college. Ten years later, when she met and married Tony, who had 6,000 jumps under his belt, she convinced him she was serious about learning. So he joined her on her first jump. Now she instructs in North Carolina, averaging 250 jumps a year.

When I asked her how it feels to skydive, she grew thoughtful. Then she murmured, "Think about driving down a road on a cool spring day. You open the window and feel wind. It's cold and noisy. You put out your hand and either let it flop in the wind or resist the wind, or you cup your hand and play with the wind, making waves. You do the same thing in skydiving, but with your entire body.

"At 13,000 feet, the door in the plane opens and you feel the cold (four degrees is lost with each thousand feet of elevation.). Once you jump, you feel the wind's resistance and you can fight it or gracefully play with it. It's not an elevator-drop feeling. You're surrounded by a *pillow* of air, and as you turn your body in relation to it, it's almost a dance."

Skydiving equipment has evolved. Instead of round canopies, rectangular ones are used today, which give jumpers more control over the way their canopies float, and the speed at which they drop or sink. For inexperienced jumpers, a line can be rigged to automatically deploy the main canopy. Skydivers carry a reserve too, which is repacked (by law) every four months by professional riggers. And most drop zones (DZs) meet U.S. Parachute Association requirements. With a little practice, landing is no harder than hopping off a chair.

Kate's voice softens with a memory. "A cousin I love very much died after a tough battle with a brain tumor. I wanted to say goodbye, so I went for a jump. As soon as I stepped out of the plane and began my freefall, I started to cry, and I cried all the way to the ground, saying goodbye to my cousin's soul." It was significant to Kate that she could grieve her farewell through the openness of sky. It brought her a feeling of peace as if somehow, for a moment, she shared a piece of the hereafter with the person she loved.

COACH'S REFLECTION: When my daughter came home from college and casually announced, "I made my second skydive," I gulped. Even though Kate Griesser says every sport with momentum contains a little danger, something about falling from an airplane triggers a flutter in most of us.

Yet isn't Kate's description of skydiving—a sport "where you consciously choose life"—the essence of the spiritual journey? As it says in Deuteronomy, *"I have set before you life and death. . . now choose life. . ."*

Choosing life means an unwavering willingness to seek truth as your way into understanding. It's a willingness to expend whatever energy is required, holding nothing back in order to live a life that does not deny, rationalize or ignore reality. You commit to going beneath the surface of things, to examining yourself honestly, and to looking at the world *as it is* with the open-eyed appreciation of a child.

A few years ago, I wrestled with a life-altering decision related to my marriage. For months, I prayed, "Help me to know truth. I will go wherever truth takes me." As it happened, truth led me along a path I hadn't expected; one that seemed painful for a while. But today I'm grateful for the direction my life took. It's brought me to a deeper understanding of myself.

Skydivers are cushioned by a pillow of air after jumping. In our quest for truth, I believe we have a cushion as well. It's called faith. And prayer.

golf balls and fishing lures . . . .

If you want to learn golf, Mike Boring will teach you. He's been a golf pro instructor for twenty-four years. And if you're one of his buddies, he'll teach you how to fish, too. As far as Mike is concerned, the two sports—he feels passionate about both—exist in a sort of parallel universe. And for Mike, they co-exist right alongside his faith in God.

"What's the major complaint people make about fishing?" asks Mike, who looks easily a decade younger than his forty-three years. I hesitate (being a non-fisher person). "Ummm . . . it's boring?" He gives me a look. "No! The biggest complaint is 'I never catch a fish!'

"But that's because fishing is an art form. You don't just *do* it. You have to learn *how*. How to cast without a backlash. How to choose the right lure. How to read the water, and notice its color. How to assess what kind of trees are growing in the lake so you can figure out where the fish might settle. The more you learn, and then practice, the more likely you are to catch a fish. And that's when fishing is fun.

"Same with golf. You never stop learning. *I'm* still learning. And nothing stays the same. I tell my students, 'A golf course is a blank canvas and you're the artist who wants to paint a masterpiece with every swing of your club. Even if you play the same course every week, the canvas changes, depending on the weather, wind, the flow of water in the water hazards, the temperature and humidity. A golf course is never the same twice.'

"Neither is a lake. Or a stream."

Mike's enthusiasm is so contagious, I'm ready to grab a fly rod or a golf club. He's already explained that his affinity for sports was a given. His dad was a natural athlete who had a chance to play for the Buffalo Bills and the St. Louis Cardinals. "But that was before pro ball brought big money and Dad had a family to support, so he turned 'em down." He took up golf instead, and when Mike was only five he went along with his dad to the driving range. His dad was Mike's hero.

"You know what brings a golfer back to the fairway?" asks Mike.

I shake my head.

"Same thing brings a fisherman back to the stream. It's the fish that got away. It's the one good shot you hit. Even if you were ready to break your clubs on every other hole, there was that one solid whack when you watched your ball go straight down the fairway. . . and you can't forget it. You want to make that magic happen *again*.

"It's special, you know? Just being out there. Maybe, like me, you're a weekend fisherman, standing in your waders. The sun's coming over your shoulder so you feel warm, but the stream feels cool. And it's quiet. All you hear are birds. Water. The rhythm and the swish of the fly rod. It's a real Zen moment.

"Same on the golf course. A lot of times, especially if I get there early in the morning before my classes start, it's like being in church. It's tranquil. I feel at home there, the way I felt when I was a kid serving Mass for Monsignor. I feel the presence of God.

"But here's the thing about golf. And fishing. And *life*. You're never totally in control. Oh, we human beings like to think we are. We're used to taking charge of our environment, right? But see, even if you get the latest high tech equipment—and you should see the changes in golf and fishing gear in the last decade. Kids today can't believe golfers used to swing a wood that was made of real wood; everything's steel and titanium now. Even if you have the latest gear and you've studied and practiced, all kinds of things can happen to your ball *after* you hit it and while it's in the air. A sudden gust of wind. A drop of rain. Same with fish. You think you outsmarted the fish? Maybe. And maybe not."

He pauses, and I know he's remembering something else. Mike's beloved dad died unexpectedly of a massive heart attack at an early age. He was just fifty-four. For Mike, it's an eternal reminder that what you love must be appreciated. Never take anything for granted. Not in golf. Not in fishing. And certainly not in life.

COACH'S REFLECTION: Today's ads show high tech equipment that goes way beyond golf clubs. There are cell phones. Computers. Palm pilots. Satellite positioning. They're all supposed to give us more control over our lives. But as Mike learned, we can still be felled by illness, an economic turndown or something else equally unplanned. Life is never certain.

When the unexpected does come, when the wind catches the ball after you have hit it or your cast goes astray, it's good to recall King Solomon's wisdom in Proverbs 3. I try to read this passage every morning: *"Trust in the Lord with all your heart, and lean not on your own understanding."*

All the high tech gear in the world can't ultimately protect us from the unknown and unplanned. But we can strengthen ourselves by trusting that something more is behind our lives than we can see. And we don't have to understand it ourselves if we can learn to lean on the Lord.

5

LIVING IN THE MOMENT

duck blind . . . .

It amused many of his fighter pilot cronies that my husband, John Bartocci, who was Brooklyn born-and-bred, became an avid duck hunter. He discovered the sport during Navy flight training when student pilots in Kingsville, Texas had to wait around for available planes. I don't remember who introduced John to bird-shooting, but on the days he didn't fly, he began getting up at dawn to drive across the flat Texas ranch-land in our blue Ford station wagon. A borrowed shotgun rested on the seat beside him.

At first, I was doubtful. "You're *shooting* those beautiful birds?"

John explained that, within limits, hunting helps maintain the ecological balance. "Besides, Barb, it's not the shooting, it's *being there* that I like. Being part of nature. Part of God's good earth. Maybe it's a throwback to pioneer life."

"What pioneers? Your dad came from Italy in 1922."

"You know what I mean."

"Pioneers ate what they shot."

"So will I. I'll clean, cook, and eat every bird I shoot."

"Don't wait for me to cook them."

"I won't."

"Or eat them."

"Sauteed in wine with mushrooms, a duck can be tasty."

"I'll stick to chicken."

His laugh made me laugh too. "Barb, chickens are just another species of birds."

When the Navy transferred us to California in 1963, John continued to duck hunt, even though it now meant a three-hour drive to reach a duck blind. Suffused with love, I surprised him with the gift of a Labrador retriever puppy. John was ecstatic. For the next several years, when he wasn't busy with Navy duties, he trained Val to retrieve. He painted duck decoys, learned to give a good duck call, and, in winter months, painted watercolor pictures of what he saw in a duck blind.

He tried to explain to me what the experience was like. The surrounding scrub pines. The hum of insect life on the water. How it felt to see an iridescent sunrise. And the deep quiet until overhead, there was the *whoo-eek whoo-eek* of ducks as they flew in low over the water.

When we took our children to the San Diego Zoo, he leaned over a bridge that spanned a pond where ducks and geese gathered, and pointed out the different species. The green head feathers of mallards; the dark-brown heads and white necks of pintails; the red eyes and reddish heads of canvasbacks; the blue-gray heads of teals.

"For me, everything comes together in a duck blind," said John. "It's almost sacred. There's the sense of being totally alive that I feel when I'm out in nature. The chance to test my own abilities. The pleasure of watching Val leap into the water and do what a retriever does best—bring back a bird."

Though I couldn't imagine myself in a chilly duck blind, I began to appreciate more how much the experience meant to John.

By now, it was the late 1960s and the Vietnam war was at full throttle. When his squadron got combat orders, John persuaded me that the best way to spend our final weekend together was to rent a tent-camper from the Navy base, take the kids and Val, and head east to the marsh land near the Colorado River. It was, by happenstance, the last weekend of hunting season.

"You want to go *duck hunting*?" I said. I'd had a more romantic weekend in mind.

But our kids loved their dad's idea. It was autumn and the land around us was a mix of brown tones. Sandy soil was speckled with occasional rocks. Reeds waved in the marsh. A gray morning sky dissolved into pale blue. The air was cool but not cold.

John got up early, pulled on his canvas waders, and crept out to the duck blind with Val while the kids and I slept inside our cozy tent-trailer. Later in the day, we took our kids hiking through the brush. That night he played his guitar, and we sang songs around a campfire. After the children fell asleep, John and I held hands in the dark, very aware that in just one week he would be headed into harm's way.

"You didn't shoot any birds," I said.

"Nope. Didn't need to." He put his arm around me. "I was happy just to *be* there. To watch the ducks fly in. To be outdoors with our kids. There's so much I want to show them. Teach them. Do with them as they grow up. I hope—"

His arm tightened around me. "I hope I'll be here to do it."

Neither one of us knew that within a year, John would be a casualty of war, his plane exploding and sinking in the South China Sea.

The night sky blazed with stars.

"I love you, Barb."

My throat tightened. I couldn't speak. I simply squeezed his hand.

COACH'S REFLECTION: It's easy to forget the true simplicity of things in today's chaotic, "24-7" world. Physical activity in the wilderness has particular value because it takes us away from modern life's instant messaging. It returns us to life at its most meaningful, where it is also profoundly simple.

In my family's memorable weekend, John was happy to just "be" and to augment his experience in nature by including his family in it—the people he loved most. Any time we focus on simply *be*-ing I think we're helped to connect with the larger reality of God.

Do you find it hard to make space in your life to simply "be" for a few hours? I know it's difficult for my daughter, who's now grown and a busy working mom. Yet even a single afternoon in the outdoors is surprisingly rejuvenating. When you do get outside, pray to be more reminded of life's fundamental simplicity. Oh, and if you can, leave your cell phone at home.

floating the river . . . .

The first April that I lived in Kansas City, neighbors invited me and my three children to go on a float trip. "Yes," I said eagerly. Then I asked, "So, what *is* a float trip?"

Their laughter was tinged with astonishment. They couldn't believe I didn't know. But in California, where I had lived before, water meant a trip to the Pacific Ocean. To Midwesterners water meant a trip to a lake or river.

And, explained my neighbors, southern Missouri is riddled with clear, fast-flowing rivers leading down to the Ozarks. They have names like The Current, Jacks Fork, Elk, White, Black, Niangua. Most are created by great natural springs, and when you stand on their banks, you are able to see nature as the early explorers must have seen it. You can imagine the fur traders, native tribes and missionaries as they stood on the same riverbanks or pushed off in canoes. "That's what we'll be doing," said Steve, who had organized the trip. "We'll be canoeing—or floating—down the Current River."

"I've never paddled a canoe," I worried as a local renter delivered eight aluminum canoes to our campsite the next weekend. "Don't worry. It's a piece of cake," said Steve. He handed me two paddles. "Here. You and your daughter can share this one. Go ahead, now. Get in. Barb, you sit in back and steer. Allison, you sit up front and help paddle. And you—" he pointed to my eager, tow-headed boys, ages ten and eight. "You two can paddle a canoe by yourselves."

"Yippee!" shouted my oldest son John. Before I had a chance to call, "Wait, are you sure it's safe?" John and his younger brother Andy were grabbing life jackets and paddles, and piling into another canoe. With feverish abandon they plied their paddles and promptly got their canoe turned the wrong way, so they were floating backward down the river.

"Don't worry," said Steve. *He sure likes that phrase*, I thought. "Even if they tip, the river isn't deep. Not here, anyway." I noted his addendum, but the boys had already managed to turn their canoe the right way, so I took a deep breath and climbed into my own stern. "Don't tip us over," warned Allison from the bow. "You *know* I don't want to get my hair wet." (Have I mentioned that she was thirteen?)

The Current is one of the first of the National Scenic Riverways. In the summer, it's so popular there are waterway traffic jams and the air is filled with noisy boom boxes. But now, in early April, we drifted downstream in near silence. A few bird calls. Laughter from farther down the river that sounded like my boys. The splash of paddles now and then.

Depending on the breeze and river currents, we would "float" or paddle twenty-five miles, then return to our camp site in a bus provided by the canoe renters. Steve and his wife Dee had a sandwich-filled cooler in their canoe for our lunch break on a sandbar.

As we paddled down river, I saw bluffs and pine forests. A blue heron swept through the water, and a funny little animal that I learned later was a mink scampered up a riverbank.

"Mom, look," said Allison. We were floating past a cave, a dark, yawning hole carved by erosion into the bluff. I would have liked to stop—two of our group had pulled up their canoes—but before I figured out how to back-paddle, we had drifted on down river.

But I knew we'd see others. Missouri is pockmarked with more than five thousand of them.

Sure enough, nine miles down river, we reached Round Spring Cave. To me, it looked like the wide-open mouth of a great fish. I even fancied I glimpsed teeth. "Mom, let's stop!" This time we managed to beach our canoe, and walked up a sandy hill with other members of our group. Inside the cave, the damp cool air reminded me of my granddad's root cellar. Allison pointed her flashlight. The stalagmites and dolomites glowed in pastel hues of yellow, purple, green. It was quite beautiful.

Back on the river, we drifted past pine forests. Saw an occasional patch of wild flowers. Once, I thought I saw a white tailed deer, but before I could cry, "Look!" it was gone.

We caught up with John and Andy at lunch. With lots of good-natured bantering, most of our group gathered on a graveled sandbar to eat sandwiches and drink Cokes, or—to me, the best of all—good cold water from canteens. The water was still too chilly for swimming, but the younger kids pulled off their shoes and waded, looking for frogs.

I clambered from the sandbar up the riverbank, and wandered by myself into a grove of trees. The sun parted the leafy branches in such a way that I felt surrounded by a circle of light. I could see the river, but the sandbar had receded from view, and the voices of my friends had blurred into indistinct sound. Gradually, I heard only the river.

living in the moment

The previous eight months had been challenging. It had been five years since my husband had become a casualty of the Vietnam War. I had returned to college, then accepted a job with Hallmark Cards in Kansas City, and was struggling, along with my kids, to adapt to our new environment. Often, I was lonely, and I worried about my children.

These were the thoughts that drifted through my mind as I stood in the grove of trees. And then—how do I explain this? The circle of sunlight seemed to grow brighter, the way stage lights will go from dim to bright, and my skin felt warmed, as if a shawl had wrapped around my shoulders. As clearly as if spoken aloud, I seemed to hear these words: "*All will be well*," and for an instant, linear time no longer existed. I felt as if explorers Lewis and Clark were around the next bend because there was no future, no past, only a circle of history, like the circle of light, and in that circle were my ancestors, my dead husband, my unborn grandchildren, and I no longer needed to worry. I felt lovingly reassured and as I asked myself, "By whom?" I knew. By God.

All will be well.

And then, "Mom! Mom! Where are you?" As my daughter's voice reached me, the moment—it had been only that—was over. I turned to see my kids coming into the grove of trees. John, ever the exuberant one, grabbed my arm. "This is so cool, Mom. I *love* float trips. You gotta watch me paddle. I'm going to get my own canoe."

"Me, too! I get to own a canoe, too."

I ruffled Andy's hair. "I don't think any of us is going to buy a canoe. But I agree with you, John. Float trips are cool. Come on, let's get back on the river."

COACH'S REFLECTION: In the years since our float trip, whenever I get scared or worried, one way I calm myself is by repeating the words I heard in that instant on the riverbank. I call them my sacred river words. *"All will be well."*

Chungliang Al Huang, in *The Tao of Inner Fitness*, says that incredible power is available when we become aware of and align ourselves with the flow of nature and the way things happen. Often it's a way that is beyond our control.

Nature's flow allowed me to reach a place, both geographical and spiritual, where I tapped into—what? A deeper part of myself? The spirit of God within me? Isn't it one and the same?

hiking new trails . . . .

"Nature is like a tonic," says Dorothy Gray, a slim blonde third-grade teacher in her early forties. "You don't need exotic locations. You can experience Mother Earth's healing energy anywhere you are."

One winter's night, feeling tired after a day of teaching, she pulled on her coat and went out to lay on the ground in her back yard in Wichita, Kansas. "As I looked up at the stars, I felt powerful energy coming through me from Mother Earth, and my weariness went away. I got up revived."

Dorothy's heightened sense of nature evolved in the wake of loss. Her ten-year marriage ended, and like most divorces "felt pretty earth-shattering." When a friend invited her to go hiking in southern Utah's canyon lands, Dorothy eagerly accepted.

They camped at Lake Powell, a glittering expanse of water whose two thousand miles of shoreline weave in and out among ancient red-rock canyons. Dorothy loved the massive rock monoliths, the house-size boulders, the rock-strewn ledges. Her inner turmoil subsided as she watched clouds at sunset turn orange and lavender, then darken into night, with stars in awesome number flung against the sky. In a way she had never experienced in church, she felt intensely aware of the creative power that is in the universe.

For the next several summers, when her children went to visit their father, Dorothy went back to Utah and Colorado. On one hike, she and three friends clambered up a 300-foot cliff. The Colorado River wove snake-like far below them. In late afternoon, as they started down, they came to a steep V-shaped crevice. At the bottom was a narrow ledge less than three feet wide. The sandstone was slippery and there were no handholds, but to go around the V meant adding another hour to their hike. Dorothy swallowed hard. If she slipped and missed the ledge, she would plunge to the river hundreds of feet below.

A friend went first, sliding his way down with the help of a walking stick. "You can make it," he called. "I'd better," thought Dorothy, "There are no do-overs."

She took a deep breath. Thought about her two kids. Said to herself, "I can do this." And slid down the V in a scattering of loose pebbles.

Looking back, she still feels empowered by the way she conquered her fear.

Her hikes led her into reading Eastern and Native American writings, which further encouraged her to connect with the nurturing she found in the natural world.

"Once, on a trail," said Dorothy, "I came to a big old elm tree leaning at an angle. I was at another cross-roads in my life, and pretty stressed. I leaned back against the tree, and it was so strong and supportive. I felt as if it spoke to me, giving me a message from the universe: *'There is plenty of help for you. You will find what you need to lean on.'* The sun was warm on my face, the birds were chattering, the tree bark was rough against my skin, and I began to sob. But when I walked on, I felt renewed, just as I'd felt when I lay against the ground that winter night."

COACH'S REFLECTION: Her hiking led Dorothy in a spiritual direction different from her formative religious experiences. I had a similar experience after I was widowed in my twenties. I enlarged my understanding of God. Though I still love and honor my religious roots, I've come a long way from the cloistered, pre-Vatican II Catholic I once was.

In his timeless book, *The Road Less Traveled*, M. Scott Peck says that spiritual growth is a journey which may mean revising—or remapping—our earlier understanding of God. We need to define God for ourselves, and not merely borrow our parents' definition.

When Dorothy enlarged her view, she did it by connecting more deeply with nature. There she found a new understanding of the supernatural. To live God consciously is a call for all of us. How is your religious view today similar or different from your parents'?

play time . . . .

I saw him again, the guy riding his tandem bicycle with a life-size skeleton perched behind him, the bones bouncing to some hard-rock music thumping from a boom box. Following him was the tattooed couple—I'm talking a *lot* of tattoos—all visibly vibrating in Iowa's humid heat as they pedaled their recumbent bikes past a cornfield. Next came a fellow on his 1896 high-wheeler

For miles and miles in either direction, all I saw were bicyclists, hundreds of them, all ages, spread out across the highway. Bearded veterans, grinning novices, a toddler in a yellow canvas bike trailer, riders on tandems, triples, racers, clunkers. Some wore team tee shirts or helmet covers: Team Skunk. Team Helen Wheels. Team INMF (It's Not My Fault). And who could miss Team Killer Bees in their yellow-and-black bicycling shorts?

I felt a surging joy. I was riding in Ragbrai, (pronounced "Rag-briy" and standing for Register's Annual Great Bicycle Ride Across Iowa) the oldest statewide bicycle tour in the United States. Two columnists for the *Des Moines Register* started it in 1973. Held every year in July, the event draws thousands of cyclists, all committed to cycling 500 miles across the state.

At six o'clock that morning, I'd wakened to the rustle of tents coming down and the sound of pedal clips clicking in place. I'd scarfed down pancakes and orange juice and been on my bicycle by 6:30.

By mid-afternoon, I had cycled past cornfields and through small towns with names like Mapleton, Lakeview, and North English. In one small town park, accordionists played polkas. Enterprising kids set up lemonade stands. The air was rich with the fragrance of sweat, manure, hogs, flowers and barbecue. Ragbrai is part county fair, part grade-school carnival, and part something more. There was a visceral sense of being in the moment and feeling the pulse—the connectedness of life.

I felt the road, smelled the cow dung, heard the starlings as they startled skyward from trees. My shirt grew damp with sweat, but if I smelled pungent, well, so did everyone else. It was all part of being there.

Five miles before our overnight stop, cheerful, sweaty cyclists stopped at the day's portable beer garden. We danced to thumping rock music, squirted water guns, and cheered a duo of lip-synching locals who called themselves "The Blues Brothers." It was Norman Rockwell overlaid with Andy Warhol.

I asked Kevin, a fellow in his thirties, why he cycled every year. He grinned. "I'm a financial analyst for a big company. *Real* stressful job. Ragbrai is my summer camp. It's my chance to play. It renews me."

COACH'S REFLECTION: *Renewal.* Through play. It makes sense. Who says spiritual renewal has to be solemn? After all, as the psalmist says, "Praise the

Lord with the harp. . . . Sing to him a new song. . . shout for joy. The earth is full of his unfailing love."

Play is a safe harbor for the soul because it's a separate reality, says Indiana University's Joseph Anderson, an expert on play. It's not "real life" so you don't have to worry about making a fool of yourself."

In play you can be silly and act in an unguarded fashion. You can test your competence, but keep risks and rewards within the play experience. A game may present the deepest theme of life—a hero struggling against difficult odds—yet cloak it in a three-hour stadium event with cheerleaders, painted faces, and rousing bugle notes *"Charge!"*

Play has a joyous quality to it because it's three-dimensional: It involves mind, body, and spirit.

So why, when there's a time-crunch, are we so quick to give it up? I see it happen in my life and maybe you do in yours. "No time for play. Got too much work to do." When we give up an activity we love because we think it's "just play" we may be giving up a joyful form of prayer. This week, give yourself permission to play. No matter how much work there is to do.

Let play be a prayer that renews your soul.

ski song . . . .

Mary Hockersmith was petite, blonde, and athletic with a college degree in physical education and a dancer's grace. She learned to ski in the Vermont mountains in the 1950s, an era when downhill skis could be seven feet long. It wasn't easy to improve your skills.

On such long boards, the art of skiing parallel—that is, turning with both skis tightly together instead of in a V-shaped snowplow position—could take a long time to learn. It was nothing like the quick shift to parallel skiing that's possible with today's short parabolic skis. Mary had been practicing every chance she got all winter.

Towards the end of February, she spent a weekend in the mountains. To help her feel the rhythm of turning—*"Pole-plant-turn"*—Mary liked to sing her way down each ski run. Her favorite was a Walt Disney tune. Plunging her ski poles into the snow, she lustily sang, "Zippity-do-*dah (Pole!)*, Zippity-*yay (Plant!)* My oh *my (Turn!)* What a wonderful *day . . . " (Pole!)* Still, the rhythm wasn't quite reaching her feet. Over and over, her long skis wrapped around each other, and sent Mary sprawling.

To make matters worse, on her final day, a nighttime storm had dumped several feet of new snow, and Mary didn't ski well in powder. By early-afternoon, she was tired and about ready to call it quits.

She decided to take one last run. But when she jumped off the chair lift at the top of the mountain, she jumped into a white veil of fog A new storm was brewing, bringing with it low clouds. The light had flattened, making it difficult to see bumps or judge changes in the terrain. It would be hard to tell where she was going, or when to turn. She couldn't even see her skis, they were so covered by the powdery snow. Briefly, Mary wondered if she should take the chair lift back down.

But that seemed like giving up, and she wasn't a quitter.

living in the moment **131**

Adjusting her goggles, she cautiously took off. The flat light was intimidating, and in the fog, her singing sounded hollow.

But as she proceeded down the ski run, something peculiar happened. Despite the difficult light, the time of day, the powdery snow, Mary's skis fell into a rhythm. "Zippity do *dah*, Zippity *yay* . . . " *pole, plant, turn . . . pole, plant, turn . . .*

Suddenly, her skis were edging together exactly as her instructor had taught. It was as if she were dancing. Though she couldn't see the tips of her skies beneath the powdery snow, she *felt* their rhythm. Her body seemed in tune with the mountain. She seemed to be floating, suffused in a kind of other-worldly light. Her skiing became effortless.

"I'm doing it!" she realized ecstatically. "I'm skiing parallel!" But in that instant of awareness, she grew self-conscious. What if she couldn't keep up the rhythm?

As soon as her ego snapped into place and she felt fear, *wham!* She tumbled and sprawled, her skis at an awkward angle.

Mary picked herself up, brushed snow off her ski jacket, reached for her ski and managed to push her feet back into her bindings. She continued down the mountain, more slowly now. *Pole, plant, turn! Pole, plant, turn!* But try as she would, she couldn't retrieve the incredible sense of union she had felt; her transcendent moment with the mountain.

Another chance to ski came along a few weeks later and Mary returned to the slopes. She continued to practice parallel skiing, and became proficient. She skied many more mountains through the years, and skiing became second nature to her. She even completed the difficult instructors' course at the Vail ski school.

But she never forgot the exhilaration of that moment in Vermont when—*zippidy-do-dah!*—she got it! The rhythm was hers! She was shushing, turning, floating, flying down the ski run, completely in touch with nature and God and the universe. Transcending her ego-self, her skis turning this way and that, in blissful, joyful, glorious rhythm, dancing with the mountain. And in a way, dancing with God.

COACH'S REFLECTION: A moment of spiritual awareness can be fleeting because our egos kick in so fast. Mary's story illustrates that truth perfectly and also shows the importance of continuing the practice. "The minute my ego snapped into place, I lost it," she said.

Have you been there? Whether you swim, run, surf, play tennis—have you been there? In the zone? In the transcendence?

As it is in athletics, so it is in prayer. There are moments of exhilaration when you are 'in the zone' and you feel the presence of God intensely. And there are other moments when your mind is ratcheting every which way and you don't feel spiritually centered at all.

Yet author Richard Foster reminds us: "Never wait until [you] feel like praying. Prayer is like any other work (or exercise) and prayer muscles need to be limbered up a bit. But once at it, you begin to feel like it. And as you practice any discipline, the moments when you sense yourself in union with the universe will increase."

simply fishing . . . .

The Missouri lake glittered beneath the morning sun. Even with his ball cap shading his face, Gary Dickerson squinted as he lifted his arms and sent his fishing line spinning. It fell in a long, leisurely arc across the water, dropping his spinnerbait lure just below the surface. Gary settled back in his fourteen-foot aluminum boat and smiled at his wife, Sue. Her line was already in the water.

It was quiet on the lake. Peaceful. He heard a soft splash as a fish jumped. In the distance, a boat motor rumbled, like someone clearing his throat. Probably a forty-horsepower motor like his. Some people liked to fish in one of the new, fancy, two hundred-horsepower bass boats, but experienced fisherman kept it simple. Simple was one of the things Gary liked most about fishing. When he threw out his fishing line, it was like throwing his problems overboard. Turning 'em back to God.

In his own life, he'd had his share of pain and disappointment, a lot of it self-inflicted. Alcohol had ruined one marriage. He'd lost a job. After he brought God into the picture, though, he'd found strength to make some changes. Maybe it was why he felt so confident about this marriage.

Sue smiled at him. No need to break the silence. The water lapping against their boat was like God talking, and Gary didn't figure to interrupt God. He glanced skyward, remembering an eagle he had seen a few weeks ago. Something about an eagle's outstretched wings made your own spirit soar. What was it Isaiah wrote? "Those who hope in the Lord will renew their strength. They will soar on wings like eagles. . . ."

"I've got a bite!" cried Sue.

Suddenly alert, she sat up straight and began to reel in, playing the bass just as he'd taught her. Gary watched proudly. When they'd met, she knew how to fish for walleye up in northern Minnesota, but fishing for bass was different. Different techniques. Early mornings, he showed her how to place her lure on top of the water or just below the surface. At midday they'd hug the shoreline in the boat, trolling beneath fallen trees and bushes. At dusk, he went back to morning methods.

It had taken some persuasion to convince Sue they should throw back most of their catches. *Leave the bass in the lake for our grandkids*" was Gary's motto. "Catching is more fun than eating," he said.

He'd even thrown back the 11.5-pound bass he caught in California, although he mounted a reproduction of it on his den wall. "This fish is bigger than my baby granddaughter," he'd crowed when he pulled the bass into the boat. What a moment that was!

Suddenly, Sue muttered, "Darn! He got away!"

"Never mind," said Gary. "Remember—"

"I know." She chorused along with him, "There's always a *next* time."

It was another thing he liked about fishing. Always a next time.

Fishing expeditions had strengthened the bond between Gary and Sue. Being on the lake made it easier, somehow, to share confidences. He told Sue his thoughts, shared his concerns, confessed to worries that he might have kept hidden on dry land. And she confided in him. He hadn't known how to do that in his earlier relationships.

Gary rewound his line and got ready to cast again. He felt a lot of gratitude these days. "Those who hope in the Lord will renew their strength. They will soar on wings like eagles. . . ."

Yep. He lifted his arm and watched his line soar across the water.

COACH'S REFLECTION: All of us make mistakes, so all of us need what Gary calls, in fishing terms, "a next time." It only works, though, if you have learned something from the past time. I was impressed when Gary said he communicates with Sue in a way he didn't know how to do in earlier relationships. It means he has learned.

Like Gary, I've learned to communicate better. I'm quicker to recognize when I'm hearing in my head "old tapes" instead of an actual communication. I've figured out what pushes my hot buttons, so in conflict situations, I can choose my response instead of emotionally reacting. I've become a better listener and am less prone to interrupt. Looking back, I wish I'd known earlier what I know now.

But we learn our lessons when we're ready to learn them. What matters is the willingness to keep learning. To keep asking the Lord to renew your strength. To have faith that there will be a next time. A time in which you will truly, in those beautiful words of Isaiah, ". . . soar on wings like eagles."

surf's up! . . . .

In Genesis it is written "The Spirit of God hovered over the waters," and Clive Farrow says it's that spirit he feels every time he's on his surf board. Clive is a tall, rangy airline pilot in his early forties whose passion is surfing. I have come to the Pacific Beach pier in San Diego to watch him.

It is just past sunrise as my eyes sweep the horizon. There! In the water! I spot them! A half dozen surfers, sleek as seals in their wet suits, patiently sprawled on their boards as they wait for the right wave. One of them is Clive.

Overhead, pink streaks are dissolving into blue. Gulls wheel in endless circles, rousing the world with their cries. The air smells of salt. Waves, small blue pillow hills, are barely frothing as they touch shore. But soon they'll build. I shade my eyes with my hand to watch.

Clive says the ocean's unending horizon offers him a natural sense of the infinite. And surfing is a *pure* form of exercise. You're not changing anything in nature. You're simply utilizing what you find. There's a sense of timelessness as you wait for the perfect wave. It gives you a chance to think, and sometimes to see your life in a larger perspective.

When you spot a wave coming, though, you pay attention. You rise in one fluid motion, like a cat arching its back. You feel the sun, warm on your skin, and at the same time, the cool sting of water. And then

living in the moment   **137**

you're up, up . . . *up* as the wave builds. Now you're going with it, whooshing down a wall of water, and it's like shushing down a ski slope except your mountain is moving, and you have to move along with it, keeping your balance, staying in rhythm.

"I feel completely *alive* when I surf. I am *in the moment*. At one with everything around me. It's enrapturing."

Clive came to surfing late—in his twenties—when he was stationed in San Diego as a Navy pilot. It was challenging to learn, but he watched other surfers and "once you get the concept mentally, your body figures out what to do."

The classic surfer's wave is called a *reef break*. It's the kind you find in Hawaii that shapes up fast because the underlying reef is shallow. It's a wave that has traveled thousands of miles, all the way from Japan or New Zealand.

"Think about it," says Clive. "The water is in motion, moving on its long journey through the ocean, and then—in a moment—it crests and it's over! It reminds you, doesn't it, of the mystery of nature and of the way things work?"

His words capture me. I picture the long, long journey of a wave-in-the-making, and then—how quickly yet grandly, it culminates and ends. It's like the ancient Chinese Taoist wrote: *"Life comes without warning and as suddenly goes."*

COACH'S REFLECTION: *"I feel completely alive and in the moment. At one with everything around me."* What a powerful statement.

When did you last experience Clive's feeling of being uplifted *in the moment?* A friend who owns a small farm said he felt it while chopping wood on a red-leafed autumn afternoon. I've had such a moment on my bicycle.

Michael Murphy, who writes so well about sports and mysticism, says, "Sport invites and reinforces an ever-deepening attention to the task at hand. . . and by quieting the surface mind can lead to moments that resemble religious ecstasy."

Not every moment will be an ecstatic one. But are you paying enough attention to the small happy, funny, or touching moments in your life? Those moments can't be retrieved. They slip through our fingers like grains of sand and are gone.

Remember: *Life comes without warning. And as suddenly goes."*

It's important to live consciously. To be aware.

To catch the wave.

wilderness walk. . . . .

At Harper's Ferry, West Virginia, Imogene Thiesen pulled on her thirty-pound backpack, grunting at the weight, and wondered—briefly—how she and Alice Lavender would get along for thirty days. It was September, and they were starting a month-long hike south down the Appalachian trail. Two fifty-something women who were—sort-of—in shape. It was Alice's idea, although Imogene embraced the adventure. Still, just because they were friends didn't mean they would hike well together.

They started out, their boots scuffling the dirt along a narrow trail that wound through a tunnel of green. It seemed a good omen to Imogene that she and Alice walked at the same steady pace.

The Appalachian trail is America's oldest and most popular, meandering two thousand miles from Maine to Georgia. At first the days were sticky-hot. Imogene's shoulders and legs hurt. But she didn't complain, and neither, she noticed, did Alice. They divided their camp duties without friction, and both were cheerful "morning people" who got up and were underway early.

Most days they hiked between seven and ten miles. Unlike the upstart Rockies, the Appalachians are old mountains, mellow in their pitch and roll, so you never hike above timberline. Imogene began to feel life's interconnectedness; how everything works in harmony. Her muscles, propelling her forward. Her heart, beating to the rhythm of her strides. Her breath, deepening as she climbed. The welcome taste of thirst-quenching water. The dappled tree-shadows, shading them from sun. All part of one whole.

Once, when the trail emerged from a sheltering tunnel of trees to cross a road, Alice blinked in the sudden bright light, then laughed. "This must be how small animals feel, emerging from their holes into sunlight."

Life lost its customary frantic edge. With no agenda, other than to reach a campsite by nightfall, there was no reason to hurry up and say something. Their conversation was leisurely. They shared childhood memories; things Imogene hadn't thought about it years.

Sometimes, they lapsed into companionable silence. Wilderness walking led easily into a meditative state.

Each lift of the foot, each folding of the knee, hands swinging loosely at their sides, the movements repeating through the hours and miles. Yet it was mind-*ful*, not mindless walking.

Imogene noticed her senses had sharpened. She stayed alert to rocks or roots along the trail, a tree's branch brushing her face, a log to climb over. She looked for the tucked-away wild flowers, the scurrying squirrel. She heard small rustles, and felt the tickle of sweat on her skin.

They met other hikers, and Imogene enjoyed the easy camaraderie. Often, they camped near people they had walked with during the day. Everyone wrote in the Park Service journals left open at the campsites. One entry said, "I'm addicted to walking. What do people *do* who don't have a day's walk ahead of them?"

Life spiraled down to its basic shape. Walk, eat, drink, sleep. Bodies grew stronger. Back packs felt lighter. Air grew brisker. One night, it got so cold, the two women skipped dinner and simply crawled into their sleeping bags to keep warm. Later that same week, it rained, two miserable days of mud and soggy tents. But the sun came out, and Imogene's soul lifted, like the hawks they saw now and then, soaring high above them. How simple life was.

COACH'S REFLECTION: I particularly like this story because it shows two very ordinary women engaged in exercise that all of us do—walking. What makes it special is where they walked and how *mindfully* they walked.

Not everyone can take thirty days off, but what about a weekend? Even a day? Like a deep breath taken in the middle of a long run, retreating to a forest—or any quiet place—can offer a spiritual second wind, and provide the solitude that makes it easier to practice more conscious living.

If you can't take any time off, try this: for one hour, *stop* multi-tasking! Instead, pay attention to the task at hand. Don't think about something else. Do whatever you're doing with a focused awareness. As the Zen master said: "What do you do after enlightenment? You chop wood and carry water." In other words, you go about your ordinary daily tasks, but with a new perception of what life is all about.

6
REACHING YOUR PEAK

golfing in the zone . . . .

No one in this book is ordinary because all of us are wonderfully unique individuals. But most of the people I talked to are amateurs in the sports world. Jane Blalock is different. She was a top player in the LPGA (Ladies Professional Golf Association) circuit and one of the first to top a million dollars in career earnings. I met her because we both belonged to the same college sorority.

Jane is retired now from LPGA play, but she's still involved with golf. She runs a Boston-based company that puts on golf events worldwide. And she was a founder of the LPGA golf clinics, which help women become more at ease with golf as a sport *and* as a business tool.

When I asked her if she sees a connection between the physical and the spiritual in her golf game, she didn't hesitate to answer.

"Absolutely. Golf requires concentration. You need an inner fortitude to stay calm in difficult circumstances. You have to overcome obstacles. A golf hole may be a dogleg, which means you can't see the green from the tee. Wind and weather may change a green's lie from what you expected. So you need resilience and perseverance. Those are all spiritual qualities— and the qualities we need to live life well.

"Golf is also a drive for perfection even if you never completely achieve it. To me, a spiritually-based life is like that, too."

Jane grew up Catholic, although today she says she's more likely to worship in "outdoor pews." She feels God's presence strongly when she walks along the course at Pebble Beach, where twisted pines stand silhouetted against Pacific waves crashing on rocks. She feels the same strong presence on one of her favorite golf courses in Japan beneath snow-crested Mt. Fuji.

It was in Japan where she had a powerful experience. One I call spiritual, though Jane used the word "stirring."

Jane went to Japan to play her final LPGA tournament in the Mazda Japan Classic in Tokyo. It was November 1985. Back problems had sidelined her for a year, but now her back felt better, and she wanted to leave golf competition on her terms: as one of the top ten women golfers.

When she arrived in Tokyo, Jane felt a strong sense of being at her peak. The week before, she had represented the U.S. in an international golf exhibition, which felt very special. She was also impressed by her tour of Kyoto, whose shrines and Buddhist temples make it Japan's great religious city.

Now, in Tokyo, she woke on the day of the tournament to a landscape shrouded in fog. The golf course, one of the most difficult in the world, seemed eerily silent in the misty gray dawn. There was a surreal quality to the opaque air. As she ventured outside, Jane realized *she* felt different, too. Totally at ease despite the fog.

When she pulled out her long iron on the first tee, her mind was free of thought, and her body seemed instinctively to know how to hit the shot. As she moved to the next hole, she was intensely aware and appreciative of the natural beauty around her: the beautiful lakes, the grass, the trees. She hit her ball effortlessly.

On each hole, Jane felt centered and without anxiety. Everything seemed part of such a gentle, easy flow that she barely remembers hitting her winning shot, which was a difficult putt on the last hole. Her brother, who watched her, said later he had never seen her eyes filled with the light they held that day.

She won the tournament with a score of sixty-four—an incredible nine under par. For Jane, it was a transcendent experience and let her leave LPGA competition on the terms she had hoped for: at the top. She had always heard that when your body and mind are fully integrated, your sports play can jump to a whole new level. She believes that happened in Tokyo. Many sports enthusiasts call it "playing in the zone."

COACH'S REFLECTION: Roger Bannister, who ran the first four-minute mile said afterward, "My mind seemed almost detached from my body. There was no strain. No pain. Only a great unity of movement and aim." Michael Murphy, who wrote *Golf in the Kingdom* as well as *In the Zone* lists twelve mystical qualities that can occur in sports:

- Peace, calm, stillness
- Detachment
- Freedom
- Floating, flying, weightlessness
- Ecstasy
- Power, control
- Being in the present
- Instinctive action and surrender

- Mystery and awe
- Feeling of immortality
- Unity
- Acute well-being.

Similar qualities are part of mystical experiences that also occur during prayer. You cannot *make* a mystical moment happen, but you can establish an environment in which it may occur. Murphy says, "The athlete knows that being in perfect control is a matter more of *grace* than of will and that one can only 'do it' by letting it happen; by letting something else take over."

That seemed to happen to Jane in the events leading up to her final competitive match. It can happen to you and to me. But only if we surrender to the divine Reality that lies behind our physical world.

hoops and hope . . . .

Debbie Milbern was tall for her age, lithe and agile. She loved anything athletic, and since she grew up right before the era of title IX and the encouragement of girls' sports, she ran, pitched, and kicked with the boys. Whatever the sport, she played it with gusto—baseball, football, and most of all—basketball.

In basketball-crazy Indiana, every driveway has a basketball hoop. Drive down streets in any season, and you'll see kids outside shooting hoops. In the Milbern's driveway, Debbie practiced every day, keeping her blue eyes focused on the iron hoop. She loved how it felt to balance on the balls of her feet, stretch her arms, lift her ribcage, and watch as the ball arched up, up, and *in*, with a gratifying swish.

On the court, there was the satisfaction of defending her teammates, getting the ball away from an opposing player, and always, always, the final thrill of launching a ball toward the basket and scoring.

Not everyone talks about basketball in terms of the spiritual, yet when you're a dedicated team member, says Debbie, you feel a commitment to something larger than yourself—the team—and you are deeply devoted to your team's welfare. You learn tolerance. You accept teammates who might be different from you, who might not be persons you would pick as friends off court, but whose well-being is now very important to you. You feel a sense of purpose toward something beyond yourself.

And always, you feel *hope* for the future. No matter how well or how badly a game was played, there is always next week's game. Whatever the defeat, there is never despair, because you tell each other, "We can rise above this."

In 1969, Debbie enrolled at Indiana University. It was the era of the legendary basketball coach Bobby Knight, who led the men's teams to win after win. Women players were grateful just to have uniforms—crimson and white—and to be able to travel between schools for their games. They played for the sheer joy of playing. There were no scholarships, no crowds, none of the attention that women's basketball gets today. Not then. Not yet.

Debbie was her team's lead scorer, averaging twenty-five points per game. The team performed so well that in Debbie's senior year, they headed for New

York and the Women's Final Four. The stands in the gym at Queens' College were packed the night they played. As the team ran onto the court in their crimson and white, Debbie heard cheers, saw the scoreboard flash, felt the wood planks dance beneath her sneakers, and without a doubt, she says now, "Even though we didn't win our games, it was one of the highlights of my life." The Indiana women's team had come through many trials—months of stiff state and regional competition—to reach New York. They were proud of the journey they had traveled.

Today, Debbie (Milbern) Powers is a tenured professor of physical education at Ball State University and co-author of a popular college textbook—*A Wellness Way of Life.* She says to her students, "Any woman who plays sports gains an independence of spirit and a sense of self-worth that will carry over into the rest of your life."

COACH'S REFLECTION: Women, especially those who came of age after title IX, agree that encouragement to play sports increases self-confidence and self-worth. Physical competence can help you feel more proficient in your job, your home life, and your personal relationships. When we stretch ourselves physically, we stretch in ways that affect our whole lives.

And whether it's commitment to a team or to an idea, people lead the most fulfilling lives when they find meaning and joy in something larger than themselves. Chicago Bulls basketball coach Phil Jackson says creating a successful team is a spiritual act, one that requires all participants to forgo self-indulgence for the greater good of the team.

Think about times you experienced a satisfying sense of commitment to a greater good. Do you feel such commitment now? If not, what do you need to do to recover it?"

And consider Debbie's words about hope *"Always, you feel hope for the future."* They reminded me of something the Rev. Martin Luther King said. *"Everything that is done in the world is done by hope."*

more than baseball . . . .

Pete Albers loves baseball. He started batting a T-ball as a towheaded four-year-old in San Diego, and by high school, played varsity shortstop for St. Augustine Catholic High. But when I asked him about the spiritual connection he found in baseball, Pete grinned and shook his head.

"We used to say a prayer before every game," he said. "But that seemed like just a school ritual. To be honest, when I watched guys make the sign of the cross before batting, I used to think, *Yeah, as if God cares if you get a base hit.* God just seemed bigger than that."

But divine power, what in Pete's Catholic upbringing was called "grace," is often channeled through human beings. And when a sport—or any activity—helps the soul go beyond self-defeating limits, the physical can become a sacred path into holy transformation.

Pete found that out at Harvard.

Harvard University may be number one in most arenas, but in 1994, when freshman Pete Albers reported for practice, their baseball team was ranked 250th in a field of 258. But losing team or not, he wanted to play.

Pete is good in a number of sports. He was even junior national Frisbee champion. So I asked what he likes so much about baseball

"The rhythm," he said instantly. "The game unfolds pitch by pitch. You're in actual play only about one-twentieth of the time you're on the field, which leaves time to appreciate other players' moves and to *think* about what a player might do.

"When I played shortstop, I'd stand behind the pitcher, and try to figure out the next batter's moves if he swung—or if he didn't swing. Would he hit the ball to the right since he'd hit it in that direction the last three times? Or would he surprise us by hitting left? Should I take a step forward because he was a fast runner? I tried to get into each hitter's head, but all I could do was make an educated guess. Once the pitcher delivered the ball, anything could happen.

"Trying to figure out in advance what was coming down and then seeing if you were right made it a game within a game. It added to the fun."

To Pete, baseball also was a game of textures, smells, and sounds. The feel of dirt being rubbed into hands. The tart freshness of new-mown grass. The saddle-like smell of a baseball glove—different from the leathery smell of the seamed ball. The musty dank odor of most dugouts. Or sometimes a smell of fresh paint!

And always, the *crack* of a bat when it hit a ball. Pete could tell by the sound if it was a well-hit ball or a dud. He liked to hear the crowd's murmur, too, the random calls thrown out between pitches. "Even if fans rooted for the other team, you drew energy from crowded stands," he said.

In his first two years at Harvard, though, fans were scarce. In Pete's sophomore year, they lost twice as many games as they won.

Then, in his junior year, Joe Walsh came to coach.

Coach Walsh had an air about him. He said, "Look, it's not about how many home runs you hit or how well you catch, it's your *attitude*. Are you a player? You know you're a player when you're willing to do whatever it takes to help your team, whether it means belting home runs because that's what you do best, or sitting on the bench, and cheering your lungs out."

He respected his players and let them know it. He believed in leadership, but thought it should occur in the trenches among the players. Every step of the way, players felt as if Coach Walsh acted for the good of the team.

"I trusted him," says Pete. "When he told me I could do something, he showed such confidence that—well, I figured I *could* do it. He made the whole team feel that way."

With Walsh coaching, players honed their skills, but the greatest transformation came in their belief systems—the way they thought about themselves and their potential.

Harvard began to win games.

They went against teams where, player for player, they didn't match up—and still won. They began to beat teams that were nationally ranked. By the end of Pete's final, senior season, Harvard's baseball team had become a team made new, not by changing players, but by changing player' attitudes. And, said Pete, they had moved from the bottom of 258 teams into the top 30.

COACH'S REFLECTION: To me, part of the power of sports is in the continual affirmation that "it ain't over 'til it's over." Who can forget the 2001 World Series? Against the San Francisco Giants, the Anaheim Angels were down three games to two. But the Angels won game six in a great comeback, and they outplayed the Giants in game seven to win the Series. It was the Angels' first win in forty-one years. Fans were ecstatic.

Psychiatrist and author M. Scott Peck refers to the "miracle called grace" when things turn out right against the odds. But is it *grace?* Or what Harvard's Coach Walsh called *attitude?* I don't think names matter. What counts is that on occasion, and not only in sports, people live beyond their usual potential.

I wonder if it's because we constantly underestimate our capabilities. Researchers say the average human uses a mere fifteen percent of physical and mental potential. *Imagine!*

"We are generally afraid to become that which we can glimpse in our most perfect moments. We. . . thrill to our godlike possibilities and simultaneously shiver with weakness, awe and fear before those very same possibilities," wrote psychologist Abraham Maslow.

Have you ever had a glimpse in your own life of unexpressed talents? I agree with those who say we're called on by God to live up to our potential. Sometimes it merely requires asking for grace.

new systems . . . .

As the plane hovered above Denver, Theresa Montano, a dark-haired pretty woman, pulled on headgear, goggles, and gloves and stepped toward the open door. Bracing for this, her fifth jump, she felt thin, cold air on her cheeks, and the rush of wind. But unlike most sky divers, she neither blinked nor looked down. Instead, she cocked her head slightly and reached for her partner's hand. Once in the air, Theresa experienced every sense but one: she could hear and touch, but she couldn't see the ground below or the billowing chute above her because she is blind.

Theresa didn't learn to sky-dive in spite of her disability. She learned *because* of it. After losing her eyesight in her senior year of high school, Theresa learned to ski, kayak, rock climb, and bicycle. Sports made her believe that she could compete in college and in the computer field despite her blindness.

A rare combination of diseases caused Theresa to lose her sight in one eye when she was five. By high school, the disease had spread to the other eye, and by her senior year, she could only see light and colors. Special tutoring and oral tests enabled her to graduate.

But her tutor noticed that Theresa hated the embarrassment of walking with a white cane. So he put her in touch with the Winter Park ski program operated by the National Sports Center for the Disabled. At Winter Park, a volunteer guide skied right behind Theresa, calling out directions and instructions. She met other blind skiers who were having a great time. Soon, she stopped feeling embarrassed because she had to wear a bright orange bib that said Blind Skier.

The more she excelled on the slopes, the more confident Theresa became that she could cope with her blindness. She learned Braille, acquired a guide dog, and enrolled at Colorado State University. In college, sports were her outlet for coping with stress, and her entrée in to campus social life. She became a familiar sight on campus, pedaling from the rear seat of a tandem bicycle while her guide dog Yatzi ran alongside.

Though her newfound love of sports helped Theresa overcome obstacles, she was badly shaken in her junior year when she lost the ability to see light and color. Now her world was totally dark. For a while, she questioned everything, including God. A friend encouraged her to try rock climbing, thinking it might lift her out of her depression.

Theresa began her first climb up a rock face near Boulder, Colorado. She had learned the basics and was roped between two experienced climbers. It was hot, sweaty, tough going, but Theresa managed foothold after foothold, beaming at each success. She reached for her next toehold and—her foot missed! With a shriek, she fell. Arms flailing, her body dangled in midair, held only by a rope. "You're okay!" shouted an instructor. His voice guided her back to the rock face.

It was scary but exhilarating. "Climbing made me realize you can't go back. Not on a rock face. Not in life. I had to keep going forward."

Theresa graduated with a degree in computer science and carved out a successful career. Occasionally, when she felt hampered by her blindness, she repeated to herself the advice she'd heard from a blind friend she met after high school. "When you lose one faculty, you don't give up. You just figure out another system that's all. And you work with one challenge at a time."

COACH'S REFLECTION: After losing one of her five senses, Theresa found sports helped her find—and use—*new systems*. They helped her discover a strength she didn't know she possessed. One challenge at a time.

When I interviewed Theresa originally for a magazine article, I was very taken by her phrase "new systems." After all, who doesn't have some disability? Some are simply less visible than others. Theresa didn't talk about prayer. But to me, prayer is more than words. It's faith in a reality that goes beyond what we have previously experienced. I felt as if Theresa lived her prayer by exercising faith in *new systems*.

When you feel overwhelmed by a problem, maybe you'll borrow, as I have, Therese's idea. Ask: "What *new system* can I use to solve this?" Maybe your answer will be "prayer."

reaching the summit . . . .

Lorry Waugh grabbed the edge of a large, imbedded rock. Using it as ballast, she pulled herself up the last steep part of the trail. Ahead of her, her son Jonathon cried, "Look, Mom, isn't it beautiful?" Eager to show off all he had learned at Boy Scout camp in New Mexico, Jon had led their two-day hike.

Now Lorry stood beside him at the summit, breathless. Partly, it was the physical exertion, but mostly, she felt breathless from a sheer sense of awe. They were standing at 12,400 feet above sea level, and all around her, she saw mountains upon mountains upon snow-covered mountains. She felt as if she were gazing at eternity. It was a deeply prayerful moment. *What wonders Thou has wrought*, she thought.

A few days later, she flew home to Pennsylvania. But she couldn't forget her experience with Jonathon. The Waughs enjoyed outdoor activities, and had encouraged all three of their Eagle Scout sons in scouting. Why not encourage other kids, especially girls? After a few days of talking it over, she and her husband Bill volunteered to lead a coed Explorer post.

The very next summer, they took forty scouts into the same mountains near Cimarron, New Mexico where Lorry had climbed with their son.

Several of the scouts had never even seen such high peaks, much less tried to climb them. In the lower elevations, where pinion trees smelled pungent and they could hear the rushing water made from melted snow, the teens jostled and joked with one another. But their voices held an edge of nervousness, and as they climbed higher, leaving trees behind, they fell silent. Boots clicked against the rocky trail. The high country air was thin and everyone concentrated on breathing and finding handholds along the steeper trails.

"It was a challenge for some of the kids," Lorry remembers, "but every one of them reached the summit." As she watched their faces, looking as awestruck as she had felt the year before, Lorry experienced an exhilarating sense of joy. *"Thank you, God. Thank you for using my legs and feet to bring these kids to this place."* She smiled at her husband and he smiled back. In that moment of shared delight, both of them knew they wanted to lead more trips.

In the next thirty years, Lorry and Bill led hundreds of kids into the mountains of New Mexico. When Bill retired a few years ago, they moved to Taos. Still trim and vigorous at seventy, they continue to hike every chance they get. And they still lead groups of young people.

Lorry told me the story of Beth, a recent hiker. At fourteen, Beth was out of shape and scared. Her parents had pushed her into the hike, hoping it would raise her self-esteem. But Beth just wanted to go home. As she whimpered, "I can't do it," Lorry's cheery voice called, "Beth, come here. I want you to walk right behind me."

Lorry had noticed Beth's fear. Now she patted her hand "You *can* do it," she said quietly. "Stay behind me and take it one step at a time. And put a song in your head, something with a good rhythm. You know what I sing?" She chuckled. "'The old gray mare—she ain't what she used to be.'"

Beth couldn't help it. She laughed. "You really think I can do it?"

"I *know* you can. And won't you be proud when you reach the peak!"

It was a tough climb for Beth. More than once, she gulped. Once she shrieked, "I'm going to fall!" But Lorry's quiet, good-humored voice continued to encourage her.

When they did reach the peak, Beth stood breathlessly for a moment before turning with a luminous smile toward Lorry. "I did it," she whispered.

Lorry said a silent thank you. Once again, God had used her legs and feet to help someone reach the summit. Then she smiled. "I *knew* you would, Beth."

COACH'S REFLECTION: The idea of leading—and being responsible for—a group of teenagers as they climb a mountain leaves *me* in awe. I can't imagine doing it. Lorry and Bill are excellent examples of the way we express our connection with God through physical activity. But it's more than the activity itself. A spiritual connection depends on the *intent* we bring to exercise.

When she shared her love of the mountains and encouraged young people to make their own journeys of discovery, Lorry felt as if she acted as "God's hands and feet." Her sharing intent deepened her own pleasure in her climbs.

She also saw how achieving a summit became a true peak experience for kids like Beth, helping them see themselves differently. And how did Beth achieve her goal? The way all of us do, step by step.

Whatever your exercise, if you want to bring to it your best energy, take a moment before you begin to consciously state your intent. When you do that, author Gabrielle Roth says you "sweat your prayer."

sacred skiing . . . .

As a kid growing up in Michigan, Kevin Hayes hated winter. "When I grow up, I'm moving someplace *warm*," he said. And after earning his law degree, he did. He moved to California. Then a chance to become a prosecuting attorney brought Kevin back to—yes—his home state of Michigan.

He loved his job, but how to survive winter? There was only one way, he decided. He would embrace an outdoor sport that could help him persevere through the long, snowy, uncomfortable months. He chose Nordic, or cross-country, skiing.

Cross-country skiing has an entirely different feel from shushing down steep Alpine ski runs. There are no hot dog skiers or snow boarders, no rope tows or lift lines, just quiet trails in the snow, and the satisfying aerobic exertion of moving arms and legs in sync.

For Kevin, skiing became his saving grace. Even when he was tired at the end of a long workday, he forced himself to pull on ski gear and head out along a nearby trail. Once outdoors, he felt his heart and soul stir as he drew into his lungs the crisp cold air.

Before long, he was averaging fifty ski days a year, sometimes going for just an hour after work, sometimes gliding alone on Saturday into Michigan's deep woods. There he felt powerfully the presence of God. It was almost like going on a sacred pilgrimage, where you do something for the sake of doing it, not for the end result.

It was easy for Kevin to feel a divine presence. He's one of ten kids raised in a big Irish Catholic family, and religion has always been part of his life. He attends Sunday Mass. He takes time each night to pray. In his legal work, he tries to balance justice with mercy.

He saw parallels between skiing and the beauty he found in his religion. He liked the ritual of slowly, patiently waxing his skis, the fragrant wax like a kind of incense. He kept vigil over snow conditions, and saw the sacramental traces of God's creation in the flash of white as a rabbit's tail disappeared down a hole, in the shape of an icicle hanging from a tree limb, in the peculiar light that filters through falling snow.

One day Kevin realized he'd been back in Michigan for fifteen years. He was nearing forty! He had a wife, a family, a good job—but like a lot of others who hit midlife, he craved a new challenge. He decided to test his perseverance by skiing a cross-country marathon.

Skiing a 50-K marathon with 300 other skiers is not the same as exploring the woods on your own. Kevin was used to skiing in relatively flat country. His first marathon was held near Traverse City where white hills billowed like sheets on a clothesline. Sweat pooled inside his sweater as he carefully balanced his long skis and prepared to head down another hill. It was ten times harder than he'd expected. He finished *last* in his age group.

Mortified but tenacious, Kevin skied the same marathon the next year. This time, he finished in the top half of the skiers. When he skied it a third time, he won third place overall.

"You know what I noticed? The hills that defeated me the first time I skied the course didn't even *look* like hills by the third time I skied it. It made me believe I could overcome other obstacles."

One obstacle was a fear that had held him back from fulfilling a secret dream: to try his hand at writing a novel. Writing a book is a solitary occupation requiring more than talent; you need perseverance to hang in there through the tough middle part of the book. But after all, weren't those the qualities he had called on for skiing?

"I decided, if I could do one, I could do the other," says Kevin. He finished his novel, *Kickland*, in eighteen months. His main character is a cross-country skier.

COACH'S REFLECTION: I remember a sunny winter day when I cross-country skied with a friend in Colorado. Suddenly she raised her ski poles to the sky and exuberantly shouted, "Glory to God in the Highest! And thank you, Lord, for this day!" I laughed—and privately agreed. That memory helps me appreciate Kevin's enthusiasm for the sport. I admire, too, his perseverance. What exhilaration when you finally achieve a hard-to-reach goal!

Is there a special victory in your life? Something you ached to accomplish—and did!—though at first it nearly defeated you? Did you, like Kevin, refuse to quit?

I've learned that whatever we pursue with a steadfast heart becomes easier with practice. And eventually what seemed like an insurmountable hill may look like nothing at all.

spinning wheels. . . . .

Jami Looney was the epitome of the successful woman. By her early thirties, she owned a San Francisco apartment, earned a six-figure income, and had logged more than a million frequent flyer miles. But she was constantly on the road, had no time for a personal life, and had begun to realize that the journey that counts is the journey into your own heart. Jami was successful, but not happy.

So she made three dramatic, life-altering decisions. She chose to become a single mother, and as soon as her baby daughter was born, she left her position as an international consultant to banks, and moved from San Francisco to a quieter town in Arizona.

It's not easy to reprogram your life; nor to adjust to a whole new definition of success. It takes time. You must prepare yourself to hang in for the long run. For Jami, her shift was more than geographic. She cut her income by a whopping seventy-five percent.

And it wasn't just the money. "My change in stature scared me as much as the change in my income. I had to adjust to a whole new environment where I didn't have the connections and authority I'd enjoyed before. It was hard. It hit right at my ego."

Despite beautiful dark hair and smooth glowing skin, she was also, as she puts it, "*waaaay* out of shape." She'd given up smoking when she got pregnant, and now carried 200 pounds on a five-foot tall frame. "It was a million times harder to raise a child alone than I had imagined it would be," she acknowledged, so career stress had shifted into a new kind of stress. Food helped her cope.

Her doctor warned her of the danger to her heart. "You don't want to leave your daughter an orphan," he said bluntly. But what really got Jami's attention was the evening her adored daughter Gaby toddled over as Jami sat drinking wine on her patio. Gaby pulled the wine glass from her mother's hand. "No wine," she lisped. That's when Jami knew it was time to make more lifestyle changes.

Her business experience had taught her to be a problem solver. So, just as she had once created strategic plans for banks, she now created a strategic plan for her health. What was keeping her from a healthy life style? How could she overcome the obstacles? She knew couldn't change everything at once, so she constructed a five-year plan for herself, using research gleaned from books, the Internet, and interviews with various people.

"I realized that I needed to find a way to create an underlying balance," said Jami. She started by cutting back her drinking, then slowly changing her eating habits. No fad diets. Instead, daily journaling and learning to see food in a different way.

She added meditation, sitting outside in the Arizona dawn as the sun made pink streaks against a cloudless sky, and the mountains glimmered in the distance "I get into an Alpha state pretty quickly. It's that wonderful place where you feel as if you're floating. You're relaxed but alert."

And she began to exercise. Walking at first. Then some running. A treadmill at home.

But the exercise she loved most was *Spinning.*

"Spinning" is done on stationery bicycles fitted out like ordinary road bikes. In a darkened room at an athletic club, a group of spinners follow a leader's instructions to switch gears, go uphill, decrease speed—all delivered rapid-fire, aided by music, lights; sometimes even a moving backdrop. Jami loved the exhilaration of being with seasoned riders and pedaling so fast she felt as if her legs might drop off. The zzzzing sound of spinning wheels, the flashes of light, the energetic voice of her leader—all coalesced until it was like tapping into some kind of universal energy.

When I suggested to her that some people call such universal energy *God,* Jami smiled. She's not into conventional religion and *God* is not part of her regular vocabulary. But she looks at the journey she has made and feels as if something larger than she has been part of it.

"I've tackled so many issues in the past few years, starting with changing my career and deciding to become a mother. I've learned there is a point where you need to cross the line and say, 'I'm going to be happy' and that it's always your choice. There's something inside that I can't quite explain that gives you the courage to make that choice.

"When I'm spinning and my legs are about to drop off because I'm going so fast, I feel very aware—and grateful—for the path I'm now on. I chose not to be a sad, pathetic, fat, miserable, lonely, overworked, stressed-out person. It took time. Gaby is eight now. I think she's happy. I know I am."

COACH'S REFLECTION: Spinning is great exercise—I've done it myself. It's also a great metaphor because it's one thing to spin your wheels for health; it's quite another to realize you've been spinning your wheels in life, expending energy on what may not matter most to you.

Jami made a brave decision when she chose to go in another direction. To me, her story epitomizes the truth expressed in the scriptural words: "What does it profit you to gain the whole world if you lose your own soul?" She made trade-offs, yet she's happier today for doing it.

A question all us of need to ask periodically is this one: Am I still on the right path for me? Or is my life spinning out of control? Am I living in a way that is connected with my heart space? If not, are there changes I can make? Not every change needs to be a drastic one.

yoganetics: body, breath, life . . . . .

Wyatt Townley is tall—over six feet—and beautiful, with a great sweep of dark hair. She looks like a ballerina, and in her twenties was pursuing a dance career in New York when an accident occurred that changed her life. As part of one routine, she was lifted and tossed over the heads of several other dancers.

But during dress rehearsal, the timing was off, and she was dropped. She fell straight down from a height of twenty feet, landing with an impact that broke her neck. Though her spinal cord remained intact, doctors feared she would never dance again.

"They were wrong," says Wyatt, "I did go on to have a career, but first I had to find a way of moving that would heal rather than hurt."

Wyatt found it helped her to lie flat on her back on the floor, so her spine no longer had to hold her body upright, and she was not stressing her joints. She closed her eyes, relaxed, and began breathing—long, deep breaths that filled her lungs. With her eyes closed, she didn't think about how her body *looked* or about what her future held. She concentrated instead on how her body *felt* in the moment.

Slowly she began to experience her body's interior: her muscles, spine, shoulders, neck.

As she adapted certain yoga movements to horizontal floor movements, and experienced the benefits, she began showing others how to do what she called "*Yoganetics*." Today, she is married to a writer, teaches Yoganetics and publishes poetry.

The first time I met Wyatt, I was awed by her beauty, and by something else, something I couldn't put my finger on at first. Eventually, I realized that she personifies what she calls the power of *presence.*

"Next time you go to a big party," she writes in her book *Yoganetics.* "Sweep the room with your gaze. Chances are you'll spot one or two people who stand out. The air around them feels charged and people feel energized just being near them. It's the quality of being present in your body in the moment. The more fully a person occupies his or her body, the more palpable the presence."

Many people, Wyatt observes, are *not* present in their bodies. They look at the body as simply a *thing* that follows commands ("Run faster! Lift the leg higher!") or a garment that needs altering. ("Get in better shape! Start a fitness program!"). Exercise itself seems boring so people use props—Stairmasters, treadmills, fitness machines—and distract themselves with TV or loud, thumping music.

"But if you enter your body from inside-out and work from the interior, the world you find inside yourself is exhilarating," she told me. To experience what she meant, I signed up for one of her classes.

As happens too often in a hectic life, I was running late the day of the class, and on my way over, another driver (probably as late as I was) almost ran me off the road. So I was feeling harried and irritated ("Stupid driver!") as I lay down on a mat in Wyatt's exercise room. Around me were a half dozen other supine people, including two older men. The light was dim, the room, quiet. Obediently, I closed my eyes, although my heart was still racing.

Wyatt's voice flowed over us like syrup.

"Surrender the weight of your body to gravity. Let go. The earth will catch and cradle you. Now imagine that your spine is a river. Visualize this river flowing between your head and tailbone. . . Drop your chin and lengthen the back of the neck so the river can course freely through you. . . "

Her voice continued—slow, hypnotic—leading the class through various movements. Although a few called for a sitting position, most were done with the back against the floor. As I listened to the rhythmic cadence of her voice, and lifted my legs, pulling in the muscles of my buttocks and abdomen, lengthening my spine, I noticed sensations I was normally too busy to notice. The cool smooth touch of the wooden floor against my fingers. The sound of breathing. A clock's ticking from somewhere down the hall. Gradually, a tranquil feeling began to replace the harried one I had brought with me.

"Breathe," said Wyatt. *"And feel yourself return to your natural state of grace."*

I took a deep breath and all the tightness within me let go.

COACH'S REFLECTION: Wyatt's poem, "The Breathing Field," speaks of my experience—and possibly an experience you have had—as only poetry can. Breathe slowly as you read it.

The Breathing Field

Between each vertebra
Is the through line
Of your life's story,
where the setting sun
has burned all colors
Into the cord. Step

over. Put on the dark
shirt of stars.
A full moon rises
Over the breathing field,
seeps into clover and the brown
lace of its roots
where insects are resting

their legs. Take in the view.
So much is still
To be seen. Get back
behind your back, behind
what is behind you.

how-to

KNOW YOURSELF

You've read the stories in this book about others. How they found a spiritual dimension in their exercise programs. Here are two sets of questions to help you understand your own current attitudes about physical and spiritual exercise.

What are my attitudes about physical exercise?

- Exercise is a necessary chore to stay fit.
- I make time in my life to play a sport that I absolutely love.
- I feel better when I work out.
- I know I should work out but I don't have time.
- When I do exercise, I go to a gym.
- I prefer to work out at home.
- I prefer outdoor exercise.
- I like to exercise in the morning and get it "over with."
- I like the stress relief of exercising after work.
- I do better if I have a coach, personal trainer, or workout buddy.
- I like the solitude of working out alone.
- I like to do other things while I exercise, such as read, watch TV, or play CD music.
- I prefer to play team sports.
- I prefer individual exercise
- Exercise already has a powerful spiritual component for me.
- I've been "in the zone"—had a sense of heightened consciousness—while exercising.

What are my attitudes about prayer, God, spirituality?

- I believe in a personal concept of God.
- I believe there is a larger reality in the universe behind the physical world we see.
- I believe in Jesus Christ as the Son of God.
- I attend a house of worship.
- My best "house of worship" is outdoors in nature.
- I pray daily.
- I don't pray daily but I pray with some regularity.
- Meditating for ten to twenty minutes at least three times a week sounds like a good practice.
- I don't have time to meditate.
- I talk to a spiritual director on a regular basis.
- I have a prayer partner and we regularly pray together.
- I would feel embarrassed to pray with someone else.
- I regularly read the Bible or books by spiritual writers.
- I write down my own thoughts in a prayer journal.
- Although I may read and write as part of my prayer time, I have never thought about combining prayer and exercise.
- I've experienced a sense of heightened consciousness during prayer.

- Combining exercise and prayer appeals to me because I could accomplish two worthwhile activities at once.

These questions aren't "official" by any means. But they may help you notice your natural behavior right now. After answering the questions, here are a few things to pay attention to:

- Do you prefer group worship? Have a preference for team sports? Then a solitary sport, like running, may not be for you.

- Do you like having a personal trainer or a spiritual director? This may indicate that you need to meet with someone regularly in both physical and spiritual exercise.

- Did you note difficulty in finding time for yourself, whether for exercise or for prayer? Only you can figure out a way to make the time needed. It will probably involve some very careful planning

- Do you prefer exercising while doing something else? Spiritual reading to quiet meditation? Then you might consider equipment like a stationary bicycle where you can do spiritual reading while you exercise. Or exercise and pray with the help of prayer beads.

- Did you note an early morning preference for exercise and prayer? Or at night? You're more likely to stay with a program if it's in tune with your natural body rhythm.

- Do you prefer the outdoors to indoor houses of worship? Then plan your exercise/prayer around trips into nature.

Integrity, wholeness, authenticity are words that fit anyone who wants to live a prayerful, God-connected life. Let your answers on these two questionnaires help you see your natural preferences, so you can plan a physical/spiritual exercise program that reflects the authentic you.

seven rules for sports and for life . . . . .

① Keep your eye on the ball. Make God the center of your life.

② Be a good team player. Love others as you love God and yourself.

③ Realize some games will be rained out. Not all prayer brings mystical moments.

④ Winning isn't everything. God asks only that you do your best.

⑤ Practice regularly. Learn self-mastery through regular meditation and spiritual disciplines.

⑥ Listen to the coach. Read the Bible and heed your pastor.

⑦ Play for the love of the game, not the final score. Live one day at a time. Believe God's grace is always available.

TWENTY-ONE INSPIRING WAYS
TO ACHIEVE PHYSICAL AND SPIRITUAL FITNESS

Anticipate.

While putting on your workout clothes or driving to your gym, visualize yourself doing your workout. Mentally rehearse how you'll feel: the pleasure, exhilaration, and strengthening your exercise will bring you.

Create your intention.

Spiritual masters point out that whatever we focus our attention on will command our energy. So any activity that is done with "right motive" will engage our best energy. Before starting your exercise, consciously affirm your intent to combine the physical and spiritual.

Two affirmations I like to say are these:

① "Let my spirit move in prayerful concert with my body."

② "I invite God to be with me as I exercise today."

Then, simply pay attention to the natural rhythm and flow of what you're doing.

Breathe.

Breath work is so important! Breathe deeply before exercising. Feel the air moving into your body, lifting you. Imagine that the bottoms of your feet are receiving energy from Mother Earth. As you inhale, picture that you are drawing in God's holy spirit. Pull your breath smoothly up through your torso and exhale through a relaxed, open mouth. As you exhale, picture yourself releasing negative toxins of anxiety, fear, and impatience.

Monitor your breathing while you exercise. A ski instructor asked her students to notice their breathing as they sped down a steep slope. Some discovered they were nervously holding their breaths all the way down. Keep breath flowing evenly into and out of your body *during* your exercise.

Stretch.

Stretching each morning keeps you limber and flexible, which is especially important as we grow older. But stretching does more than open your rib cage and lengthen your spine. As your body opens, your soul opens. Lift both arms high in what yoga calls the Sun Salute. Or, if you wish, let it be a salute to the Son, the word of God made flesh.

In my city, the public television station and Lifetime cable both offer 6 a.m. shows to lead viewers in yoga stretching exercises. I find it's an inspiring way to start my day.

Open your hands.

The conscious act of slowly opening your hands, palms up, signifies an act of surrender, and your willingness to open yourself to life as it *is*. Before exercising, open your hands in this slow, conscious way. Let it symbolize your willingness to receive the spiritual gifts from your bodily movements.

Repeat a mantra word.

To keep your mind relaxed, in what's known as the Alpha state, repeat a word or phrase over and over while you exercise. You can choose something secular (love or peace or calm mind-calm body). Or you might choose words from your religious heritage.

I like to say, "Jesus mercy, Christ have mercy." I know others who say the "Hail Mary." Or murmur "The Lord is my shepherd." A Buddhist might use "Om."

Another way to use repetition is to vary your word or phrase from week to week, reflecting different qualities that you want to encourage in yourself. One week it might be "compassion." Another week, "love." Another week, "forgiveness."

These meditative "mantra" words help center thoughts in a positive direction and keep minds free of chatter.

Stay positive.

Avoid negative thought processes that some experts call "chaining." You begin by worrying about your boss's critique of a report you prepared. Then you jump to the rumor that your company is downsizing. Uh-oh. What if your boss is unhappy with your work and lets you go? In minutes, you're picturing yourself as homeless and on the street! All this while jogging down a trail near your home.

Once you realize your thoughts are forming a negative chain, simply say to yourself, "*Stop*," and gently bring awareness back to what you're doing, whether it's lifting a tennis racket or paddling a canoe. Repeat your mantra word at the same time or say a short prayer.

Notice your body.

Sometimes we're stressed without really knowing why, which interferes with spiritual connections. It's a good idea to pay attention to the clues your body gives you.

In Chicago, Joelle Hogan noticed that as she volleyed a tennis ball, she was hitting it *really* hard. She asked herself why, and realized she was angry about a situation at work. By noticing her physical actions, she got in touch with her mental agitation. Then she used exercise to help discharge her feelings.

Take inventory of your body by asking, "What's happening in my gut? Is my stomach tight or relaxed? What sensations are in my chest? My back? My shoulders? What do I feel in my throat? Is my brain chattering?"

Extend yourself.

Inner power means confidence that you can handle whatever comes in life. The Psalmist says, "Be strong and take heart, all you who hope in the Lord." One way to affirm your strength is to extend yourself beyond your usual comfort zone.

The first time I bicycled, I quit after five miles. But every time I rode, I pedaled a little farther. Now it feels like nothing to cycle forty miles.

It also helps to work out with someone who's better than you. To keep up, you'll ski a little faster. Play a sharper game of handball. Run a little farther.

Vary your exercise.

The human body adjusts quickly to any repetitious exercise routine, so if you always do the same workout you'll eventually plateau. When that happens, you no longer get the same benefits from your routine. Cross-training invigorates your muscles—and your mind. I like to bicycle three times a week and swim two days. I lift weights every other day.

You might vary your meditation, too. In my Catholic growing up years, I learned to meditate on the mysteries of the Rosary. Each one depicted a different gospel scene: joyful, sorrowful, or glorious. You can vary your meditations using your own religious tradition.

Go outdoors.

Even if you normally exercise inside, add an outdoor activity now and then. Some people find it's easier to feel a sport's spiritual dimension when they're out in nature. "Nature's peace will flow into you as sunshine flows into trees . . . and cares will drop off like autumn leaves," wrote naturalist John Muir. Open your eyes to the wonders of nature.

Jump for joy.

Children are awake and alive with God. It's apparent in the way they play with such abandon and joy. They skip rope. Run. Jump. Not to burn calories. Not to achieve a goal, but for the sheer pleasure of doing it. Follow their example. Jump for joy. Or if, like me, you have bum knees, walk for joy.

Stay focused.

A powerful spiritual exercise is the practice of "The Sacrament of the Present Moment." (a phrase coined by a French Jesuit in the nineteenth century). It means surrendering yourself to God's will, moment by moment, as it unfolds in your life. To do that, you need to *notice* each moment. Instead of reading or watching TV while you exercise, pay attention to what you're doing. Use your mantra words.

Be patient.

Patience is not merely the capacity to endure, but the willingness to be at peace with whatever time it takes to reach your goal. When snags or obstacles occur, don't fight them or get discouraged. Acknowledge setbacks as learning opportunities.

Jennifer Sullivan, the director of a spiritual retreat center I like to visit, promises that regular meditation will bring positive benefits, even if you don't immediately notice them. The same thing is true when you "sweat your prayer."

Be patient, too, if you're re-starting an exercise program. Realize it will take time to get back to where you were. Don't get discouraged.

Exercise with someone else.

Part of a coach's job is to notice a player's strengths and weaknesses and to explain what needs to be worked on and how to do it. That's why it helps to exercise with a personal trainer, a coach, or a friend. If you are mixing sweat with the sacred, look for someone who has a similar intent. Neither physical nor spiritual athletes can go it completely alone.

For several years, I walked twice a week with a friend. Both of us were trying to live spiritual principles in daily life, and it buoyed me to talk to her about our faith journeys as we walked.

Use repetition.

A sport is more likely to become a spiritual experience once your physical actions become muscle memory. John Wooden, famed UCLA coach, said the road to mastery is through the eight laws of learning: Explanation, demonstration, imitation, and *repetition, repetition, repetition, repetition, repetition.* The more often you do the moves, whether it's in yoga, basketball, or another sport, the more automatically your body will respond, freeing your mind for illumination.

Talk back.

Talk back to the inner voice in your head that tries to hold you back. When you hear, "I can't do it," say "Yes I can."

"What if I hurt myself?" *"I'll take proper precautions."*

"What if I fail?" *"I'll try again."*

"It's too hard," *"Not if I break it into smaller steps."*

Listen for any voices of fear and negative thinking.

Say to yourself, "I *can* do this" and then add the wonderful line from St. Paul: *"Not I, but the Christ in me."*

Visualize.

Coaches have learned that it makes a telling difference if an athlete will visualize beforehand the moves and action planned for an actual athletic event. Whatever we put our attention on develops and grows stronger.

Visualize yourself doing a particular physical action. Picture how you would act, look, and feel if you had more stamina. More endurance. More connection to God as you exercise.

Give ninety percent.

Coach Bud Winter observed that runners who tried too hard interfered with their own peak performance. So he developed his ninety percent rule. He discovered that when runners relaxed a little and allowed themselves to perform at what they considered ninety percent, paradoxically they often ran faster. The same truth found in the Tao Te Ching: *"Practice not-doing. Everything will fall into place."*

Believe. And See.

When you combine athletic endeavor with a prayerful spirit, you may experience a shift in consciousness. In their research, Michael Murphy and Rhea White (*In the Zone*) found that sport has enormous power to sweep us beyond our ordinary sense of self. . . to evoke what is generally regarded as mystical. Though you can't *make* such an experience happen, you can be willing for it to occur.

Avoid perfectionism.

To insist on perfection is, in itself, an act of imperfection because you're attempting to achieve the unachievable. In all things, and especially in sports and prayer, you are asked only to do your best. Perfection is in God alone.

RESOURCES

As Above, So Below
By Ronald S. Miller and editors of New Age Journal, Jeremy P. Tarchers, Inc., 1992

Body, Mind and Sport
By John Douillard, Harmony Books, 1994

Bone Games
By Rob Schultheir, Random House, 1984

Care of the Soul
By Thomas Moore, HarperPerennial, 1992

Celebration of Discipline
By Richard J. Foster, Harper & Row, 1978 (1st edition)

Contemplative Creations I and II
Music CDs by Tom Jacobs.

Embrace the Tiger, Return to Mountain: The Essence of Tai Ji
By Chunglian Al Huang, Celestial Arts Press, Berkeley, CA, 1987

Faith in Sports: Athletes and Their Religion on and off the Field
By Steve Hubbard, Doubleday, 1998

Fit From Within: 101 Simple Secrets to Change Your Body and Your Life
By Victoria Moran, Contemporary Books/McGraw-Hill, 2003

Fitness is Religion: Keep the Faith
By Ray Kybartas with Kenneth Ross, Simon & Schuster, 1997

Healing Words: The Power of Prayer and the Practice of Medicine
By Larry Dossey, M.D., HarperCollins, 1993

Imitation of Christ
Edited by Harold Gardiner, S.J., Doubleday & Company Inc., 1955

In the Zone: Transcendent Experience in Sports
By Michael Murphy and Rhea A. White, Penguin/Arkana Books, 1995

Invitation to a Great Experiment: How to Start a New Way of Life That Works
By Thomas E. Powers, East Ridge Press, 1986

Leading With the Heart: Coack K's Successful Strategies for Basketball, Business and Life
By Duke University basketball coach Mike Krzyzewski with Donald T. Phillips, Warner Books, 2000

Miracle of Mindfulness
By Thich Nhat Hanh, Beacon Press Books, 1987

One Hundred Greatest Moments in Olympic History
By Bud Greenspan, W. Quay Hays, publisher, 1995

Quest for Success
By Steven Ungerleider, Ph.D., WRS Publishing, 1995

The Quotable Climber
Edited by Jonathan Waterman, The Lyons Press, 1998

Raising our Athletic Daughters
By Jean Zimmerman and Gil Reavill, Doubleday, 1998

The Relaxation Response
By Herb Benson, M.D., and Miriam Z. Klipper,
Wholecare, 2000

The Road Less Traveled: A New Psychology of Love,
Traditional Values, and Spiritual Growth
By M. Scott Peck, M.D., Simon and Schuster, 1978

Seeking God: The Way of St. Benedict
By Esther de Waal, The Liturgical Press, 1984

Self Nurture
By Alice Domar, Ph.D., Viking Press, 2000

Sport Inside Out
Edited by David L. Vanderwerken and Spencer K.
Wertz, Texas Christian University Press, 1985

Sweat Your Prayer: Movement as Spiritual Practice
By Gabrielle Roth, Tarcher/Putnam, 1997

Transitions: Making Sense of Life's Changes
By William Bridges, Addison-Wesley, 1980

Yoganetics: Be Fit, Healthy, and Relaxed One Breath at a
Time
By Wyatt Townley, HarperSanFrancisco, 2003
See www.yoganetics.com for information on video
tapes

Working Out, Working Within: The Tao of Inner Fitness
Through Sports and Exercise
By Jerry Lynch, Ph.D., and Chungliang Al Huang,
Jeremy P. Tarcher/Putnam Inc., 1998

More Meditations for Today's Life . . .

A Cup of Grace . . . To Go
What Jesus Might Say to Start Your Day
Anita M. Constance

If you've been looking for a way to spiritually fortify your daily journey, your search is ended. Offers simple, practical, time-sensitive prayer-starters to begin (or even continue or end) your day.

ISBN: 0-87793-965-9 / 112 pages / $8.95

Slow Down
Five Minute Meditations to De-Stress Your Days
Joseph M. Champlin

In today's fast-paced, work-driven, never-slow-down world, there often just isn't any time to de-stress, much less to devote any time at all to spiritual development. This book provides a way, with 101 short spiritual meditations.

ISBN: 1-893732-78-9 / 208 pages / $9.95

"Don't Gift-Wrap the Garbage"
Down-to-Earth Daily Meditations for Women
Karen Stroup

Here's a book of daily meditations written for today's women – those women that are more likely to find themselves on their knees scrubbing the bathroom floor than in prayer at a retreat house. Reflections are shared from an ordinary life from silly to the serious with spiritual tidbits for every day of the year.

ISBN: 0-87793-968-3 / 576 pages / $15.95

Loving Yourself More
101 Mediations for Women
Virginia Ann Froehle

"Love your neighbor as yourself." Many women today are realizing that they have kept the first part of this commandment too well and the second part too poorly. Virginia Froehle invites women to dwell on the most basic of all Christian truths: God's love for us and God's call for us to love ourselves.

ISBN: 0-87793-513-0 / 128 pages / $7.95

Keycode: FØSØ1Ø4ØØØØ